BEYOND WORDS

One family, three generations

BEYOND WORDS

What Elephants and Whales Think and Feel

CARL SAFINA

ROARING BROOK PRESS New York

Copyright © 2019 by Carl Safina

Published by Roaring Brook Press
Roaring Brook Press is a division of Holtzbrinck Publishing Holdings Limited Partnership
175 Fifth Avenue, New York, NY 10010

mackids.com

Library of Congress Control Number: 2018944871
ISBN 978-1-250-14463-8

Our books may be purchased in bulk for promotional, educational, or
business use. Please contact your local bookseller or the Macmillan Corporate and
Premium Sales Department at (800) 221-7945 ext. 5442 or by email at
MacmillanSpecialMarkets@macmillan.com.
First edition 2019
Book design by Aram Kim
Printed in the United States of America by LSC Communications,
Harrisonburg, Virginia
1 3 5 7 9 10 8 6 4 2

For the people in these pages who watch and truly listen,
who tell us what they are hearing in other voices
that share our air, and in the silence

CONTENTS

PROLOGUE

Another big group of dolphins had just surfaced alongside our moving vessel—leaping and splashing and calling mysteriously back and forth in their squeally, whistly way, with many babies swift alongside their mothers.

I wanted to know what they were experiencing. What is it like to be a dolphin?

My question for the dolphins was: **Who are you?**

During the cruise I'd been reading about elephants. So, elephant minds were on my mind as I watched and wondered about the dolphins living and traveling freely in their ocean realm.

That is why this book is about elephants—the world's largest land animals—and orcas, also called killer whales, which are the world's largest dolphins. This book is my attempt to answer the question of who they are.

We say "humans and animals" as though life falls into just two categories: us, and all-of-them. Yet we've trained elephants to haul logs from forests; in amusement parks, we've trained killer whales to entertain us. In this book, we will see how those creatures really live when they are being themselves in the world. We will see who they really are.

I was seven years old when my father and I fixed up a small shed in our Brooklyn backyard and got some homing pigeons. I watched how they built nests in their cubbyholes, seeing them courting, arguing, caring for their babies, flying off and faithfully returning; how they needed food, water, a home, and one another. I saw them living in their apartments like us living in our apartments. Just like us, but in a different way.

But the real question isn't whether they are like us. The real question is: Who are they, what are they like, and what is life like for them? What might they be thinking? What are they likely feeling?

I wanted a better understanding. And to get that, I needed to take us to where the animals are free-living, working for themselves and their own families.

So, come along. Get your stuff; let's go.

PART ONE

Lives of Elephants

*Delicate and mighty, awesome and
enchanted, commanding the silence
ordinarily reserved for mountain
peaks, great fires, and the sea.*

—Peter Matthiessen,
The Tree Where Man Was Born

A baby elephant curiously investigates its world

CHAPTER 1

Hitting Reset

"Look how fat *that* baby is," I say. The fifteen-month-old looks like a ball of butter. Four adults and three little babies are playing in a muddy pool, spraying water over their backs with their trunks, then sprawling on the squishy bank. It's soothing just to watch.

The elephants seem happy. But when elephants seem happy to us, do they really feel happy?

"Elephants experience joy," Cynthia Moss tells me. Cynthia is a scientist who has studied them for forty years. "It may not be human joy," she says. "But it is joy."

Elephants act joyful in the same situations that make us joyful: familiar friends and family, lush food and drink. So we easily assume they feel the way we feel. But beware of assumptions!

Understanding animals' thoughts and feelings happens to be the main quest of this book. The tricky task ahead: to go only where evidence and logic lead. And—to get it right. I am here at Amboseli National Park in Kenya, Africa, because I am ready to learn, ready to ask. How are they like us? What do they teach us about ourselves?

"What has a lifetime of watching elephants," I ask Cynthia, "taught you about humanity?" I glance to make sure my recorder's light is on, then settle back a bit. Forty years of insight; this will be good.

What I don't see coming is: I have the question almost exactly backward.

Cynthia gently deflects my question. "I think of them as elephants," she says. "I'm *interested* in them as elephants. Comparing elephants to people—I don't find it helpful. I find it much more interesting trying to understand an animal as itself."

It takes me a moment to "get" her comment. Then—I am stunned.

As a lifelong student of animal behavior, I'd long ago concluded that many social animals—certainly birds and mammals—are, in many ways, like us. I've come here to see how elephants are "like us." I am *writing this book* about how other animals are "like us." But I'd just gotten a major course correction.

Cynthia's comment hit Reset, not just on my question, but on my thinking. I'd somehow assumed that my quest was to let the animals show how much they are like us.

My task now—a much harder task—is to see *who* animals *are*—like us or not.

CHAPTER 2

Seeing Elephants

"It was the worst year of my life," Cynthia Moss is saying over breakfast. "All the elephants over fifty years old, except Barbara and Deborah, died. Most over forty died. So it's particularly amazing that Alison, Agatha, and Amelia have survived."

Alison, now fifty-one years old, is right *there,* in that clump of palms. When Cynthia—who still has bright blue eyes and a bubbly personality—arrived in Kenya forty years ago to study the lives of elephants, she came here. The first elephant family she saw she designated the "AA" family, and she named one of those elephants Alison. And there Alison is. Right there, vacuuming up fallen palm fruits. Astonishing.

With luck and decent rainfall, Alison might survive ten more years. And there is Agatha, forty-four years old. And this one coming closer now is Amelia, also forty-four.

Amelia continues approaching, until—rather alarmingly—she is looming so hugely in front of our vehicle that I reflexively lean farther into the vehicle. Cynthia leans out and talks to her in soothing tones.

Amelia, practically alongside us now, simply towers as she grinds palm fronds, rumbles softly, and blinks.

Cynthia helped pioneer the surprisingly difficult task of simply seeing elephants doing elephant things. Longer than any other human being ever has, Cynthia has watched some of the same individual elephants living their lives.

This national park—Amboseli—is actually too small for the hundreds of elephants who use it. Amboseli elephants use an area roughly twenty times larger than the park itself. The elephants come here for water. As do cattle- and goat-grazing Maasai people. The only year-round water is here. The 150-square-mile park serves as a central watering hole for the surrounding 3,000 square miles. The park is too small to feed them all. The outer lands are too dry to water them. The food is out there; the water is in here.

Just four years ago, extreme lack of rain—a drought—shook this place to its core. "To survive the drought," Cynthia is explaining, "different elephant families tried different strategies. Some tried to stay close to the marsh. But they did very badly as it dried. Some went far north, many for the first time in their lives. They did better. Out of fifty-eight families, only one family did not lose anybody." One family of elephants lost seven adult females and thirteen youngsters. "Usually if an elephant goes down, the family gathers around and tries to lift it. In the drought, they had no energy. Watching them dying, seeing them on the ground in agony..." Cynthia closes her eyes and shakes her head.

One in four of Amboseli's elephants—four hundred, out of a population of sixteen hundred—perished. Nearly every nursing baby died. About 80 percent of the zebras and wildebeests died, and nearly all of the Maasai people's cattle. Even humans died.

But when the rain returned, it triggered the biggest baby boom in Cynthia's history here. About 250 little elephants were born in the last two years. This is a sweet spot in time to be born an elephant in Amboseli. Lush vegetation, plenty of grass—and little competition. And water. Water makes elephants happy.

Several happy elephants are sloshing through an emerald spring under the shade of palm trees. They seem to have found a little patch of elephant paradise.

The elephants we're watching are skillfully pulling up grass and brush with their trunks and stuffing their cheeks, their massive molars mightily mashing away. Thorns that can puncture a tire, palm fruits, bundles of grass—it all goes in. I once stroked a captive elephant's tongue. So soft. I don't understand how their tongues and stomachs can handle those thorns. I realize I don't know much about them.

But Cynthia does. "When you look at a group of anything—lions, zebras, elephants," Cynthia explains, "you're seeing just two flat dimensions. But once you know them individually, who their mother was, who their kids are, their personalities…" One elephant in a family might seem regal, dignified, gentle. Another will strike you as shy. Another as a bully who will be pushy to get food in sparse times, another as reserved, another as exceptionally playful.

Cynthia continues, "The realization of how complex they are took me about twenty years. Over the period that we were following Echo's family—she was about forty-five years old at the time—I saw that Enid was incredibly loyal to her, Eliot was the playful one, Eudora was flaky, Edwina was unpopular, and so on. And slowly I realized that I'd begun knowing what would happen next. I was taking my cues from Echo herself. I was understanding her leadership—as her family was understanding it!"

Cynthia adds, "It made me realize how totally super aware they are."

I look at the elephants. Super aware? They seem oblivious.

"Elephants don't *seem* aware of details," Cynthia explains, "until something familiar changes." One day a cameraman working with Cynthia decided that for a different angle, he'd position himself *underneath* the research vehicle. The oncoming elephants, who usually just passed by the vehicle, immediately noticed, stopped, and stared. Why was a human under the car? A male named Mr. Nick snaked his slithering, sniffing trunk under there to investigate. He was not aggressive and did not try to pull the man out; he was just curious. Another day, when the vehicle appeared with a special door designed for filming, elephants came exploring, actually touching the new door with their trunks.

The trunk is an elephant's *Swiss Army* knife. Rounded on the outer edge, flattened on the inner, a great vacuum-sweeping, water-hosing, mud-flinging, dust-deviling, air-testing, food-gathering, friend-greeting, infant-rescuing, baby-reassuring caterpillar of a nose. Yoshihito Niimura of the University of Tokyo offers: "Imagine having a nose on the palm of your hand. Every time you touch something, you smell it."

Now, they're firmly wrapping those wondrous noses around tall grass, and when the stems are strong, they give a little kick to break them. The food is freed and lifted. Sometimes they shake soil from roots. The eating is slow, relaxed.

I'd love to know how much overlap there is right now between what I am sensing and what the nearest elephant is sensing. We all have sight, scent, sound, touch, taste. We can see the same hyenas, say, as the elephants do, and hear the same lions. But we, like most other primates, are very visual; elephants, like most other mammals, have an acute sense of smell. Their hearing is excellent, too.

I'm sure they are sensing much more than I am; this is their home, and they have a history here. I can't tell what's going on in their heads. Nor can I tell what Cynthia's thinking as, quietly and intently, she simply watches.

After a severe drought, a baby boom

CHAPTER 3

The Same Basic Brain

Our job: travel around in the morning, finding them as they're coming in; see who's where. The idea is simple, but there are dozens of families, hundreds of elephants.

Four rounded babies are following their massive mothers across a broad, sweet-smelling grassland. The adults, walking as though keeping an appointment, are nodding toward the wide, wet marsh where about a hundred of their friends are mingling. Families commute daily between sleeping areas in brush-thicketed hills and the marshes where much of their food is. For many it's ten miles (fifteen kilometers) round-trip. Between here and there and day and night, a lot can happen.

"You have to know *everyone*. Yes!" Katito Sayialel is saying. Her accent is as clear and light as this African morning. A native Maasai, tall and capable, Katito has been studying free-living elephants with Cynthia Moss for more than two decades.

"I can recognize all the adult females. So," Katito considers, "nine hundred to one thousand. Say nine hundred. Yes."

Recognizing hundreds and hundreds of elephants on sight? *How* is this possible? Some she knows by marks: the position of a hole in an ear, for instance. But many, she just glances at. They're that familiar, like your friends are.

Elephants themselves recognize hundreds of individuals. They live in vast social networks of families and friendships. That's why they're famous for their memory. They certainly recognize Katito.

"When I first arrived here," Katito recalls, "they heard my voice and knew I was a new person. They came to smell me. Now they know me."

Vicki Fishlock is here, too. A blue-eyed Brit in her early thirties, Vicki studied gorillas and elephants in the Republic of the Congo before getting her doctoral diploma and coming here to work with Cynthia.

Dr. Vicki Fishlock identifies an unfamiliar male against the backdrop of Kilimanjaro in Kenya's Amboseli National Park

*   *   *

Just outside the high "elephant grass," five adults and their four young babies are selecting a shorter and far less abundant grass. It's more work; it must taste better.

The grazing elephants trail a train of white birds called egrets and an orbiting galaxy of swirling swallows. The birds rely on elephants to stir up insects as, like great gray ships, they plow through the grassy sea. Light shifts on their wide, rolling backs like sun on ocean waves. They're ignoring us.

"They're not ignoring us," Vicki corrects. "They have an expectation of politeness, and we're fulfilling it. So they're not paying us any mind."

An elephant named Tecla, walking just a few yards ahead to our right, suddenly turns, trumpets, and generally objects to us. To our left, a young elephant wheels and screams.

"Sorry, sorry, sorry," Katito says to Tecla. She brakes to a stop, turning off the ignition. It appears to me that we have separated this mother from her baby. But Tecla is not the mother. Basically she was communicating to the mother, "The humans are getting between you and your baby; come and *do* something."

Mother comes running and rejoins baby, restoring order. We slowly proceed. When one individual knows another's relationship to a third—as Tecla knows who the baby's mother is—it's called "understanding third-party relationships." They know exactly who they *and everyone else* are. They understand precisely who is important to whom.

15

Monkeys and apes—primates—understand third-party relationships too, and so do wolves, hyenas, dolphins, birds of the crow family, and at least some parrots.

As the elephants pass within just a couple of paces of our vehicle, Vicki talks to them soothingly, saying, "Hello, darling" and "Aren't *you* a sweet girl." "What I find most amazing about it," Vicki sums up, "is that we *can* understand each other. We learn the elephants' invisible boundaries. Words like 'irritated,' 'happy' or 'sad,' or 'tense'—they really *do* capture what that elephant is experiencing. We have a shared experience because," she adds with a twinkle, "we've all got the same basic brain."

Many humans think that we're the only animals who experience consciousness. But that's not true. Consciousness is *the thing that feels like something*. Cut your leg, that's physical. If the cut hurts, you're conscious. The part of you that knows that the cut hurts, that feels and thinks, is your *mind*.

Consciousness is a bit overrated. Heartbeat, breathing, digestion, metabolism, immune system, growth, healing of cuts and fractures, internal timers like the one that tells your body when it's time to sleep and time to wake up—all these things run on their own, without consciousness. And during sleep our unconscious brains are working hard, cleansing, sorting, rejuvenating.

Why be conscious at all? Consciousness seems necessary when we must judge things, plan, and make decisions.

Turns out, many other animals are conscious. Many animals are superhumanly alert—just watch these elephants when anything changes. Watch what birds do. Or a dog, when a stranger comes to the door.

Science is now confirming the obvious: Other animals hear, see, and smell with their ears, eyes, and noses; they are frightened when they have reason for fright. And they feel happy when they seem happy.

"Look at how friendly these two families are being," Vicki is saying. "Elin decided to move closer to the water, Eloise agreed, then she waited as the whole group moved up. They've obviously chosen to just spend time together today."

Obviously.

What causes elephant friendships? Certain young ones like the same games. They always play together. Certain older individuals are "compatible," Vicki says. They like to sleep at the same time, eat the same kinds of foods, and go to the same places.

Scientists didn't study animal behavior until the 1920s. That's when people first noted that chickens form a "pecking order" of dominance, and that singing birds have territories they are defending. Very basic things! Those scientists were very careful to just describe what they saw, and not interpret too much. We can observe *what* an animal does. But don't—those scientists said—try to guess what she's thinking or feeling.

Then some scientists started insisting that only humans have thoughts and feelings. Not *assuming* that other animals have thoughts and feelings was a good start for a new science. Insisting they did *not* was bad science. Since then, we have nearly a century's worth of studies of animal behavior, and of how free-living animals live. Plus, we now know much more about how brains work, and the differences and similarities between the brains of humans and those of other animals.

Humans have minds and we think and feel—obviously. But believing that only humans have minds is like believing that because humans have human skeletons, only humans have skeletons. Of course, we can see elephants' skeletons. We can't see their minds. But we can see their brains. And we observe the workings of their minds in the logic of how they act, and what they're doing. So now it is scientific to ask what other animals are experiencing.

Of course, you don't always have to be a scientist to understand these things. When a dog is scratching the door, some humans would insist that we *cannot know* whether the dog "wants" to go out. (Meanwhile, of course, your dog is thinking, "Hellooo! Let me out; I don't want to pee in the house!") Obviously, the dog *wants* to go out. And if you insist on ignoring the evidence—have a mop handy.

Like humans, elephants form deep social bonds developed through deep time. Parental care, satisfaction, friendship, compassion, and grief didn't just suddenly appear with the emergence of humans. These capacities developed over millions of years. Humans inherited them from earlier animals.

But how might we get an elephant's or a mouse's sense of the world? Elephants and mice might not tell us what they're thinking. But their brains can. Brain scans show that core emotions of sadness, happiness, rage, or fear, and motivational feelings of hunger and thirst, are generated in "deep and very ancient circuits of the brain," says noted neurologist Jaak Panksepp. Animals have inherited *very ancient* emotional systems.

So, do other animals have human emotions? Yes, they do. Do humans have animal emotions? Yes; they're largely the same: fear, aggression, well-being, anxiety, pleasure.... An elephant approaches water anticipating the relief of refreshment and the pleasures of mud. When my doggie rolls on her back to prompt me to rub her belly—again—it's because she anticipates the soothing experience of our warm contact. Even when our dogs aren't hungry, they always enjoy a treat. They *enjoy* a treat.

A baby elephant and her mother

CHAPTER 4

We Are Family

At birth, an elephant weighs 260 pounds and stands about three feet tall. Most mammals are born with brains that already weigh 90 percent of their adult weight. Elephants' brains at birth weigh 35 percent of their adult weight. Humans: 25 percent. Elephant brains, like human brains, do most of their development after birth.

The basic unit of elephant society is a female-led family. An older female, her sisters, their adult daughters, and all their children live together. The family is the foundation for shared infant care and child rearing.

Usually the oldest female is the prime holder of history and knowledge. Based on long experience, this "matriarch" makes the decisions about where the family will go, when, and for how long. She serves as the family's rallying point and chief protector, and her personality—whether calm, nervous, firm, indecisive, or bold—sets the whole family's tone.

The two groups now approaching each other are each part of the family called the FBs. All mothers are keeping in physical contact with their babies by touching them with their tails. Right now their matriarch, Felicity, is leading her daughters and two females—Flame and Flossie, who are sisters. Fanny is with her young ones, her niece Feretia, and her great-niece Felicia. Vicki tells me that Felicity and her offspring are always touching one another. By contrast, Fanny is very levelheaded but not hugely affectionate with her young ones.

Fanny's group joins Felicity's. In elephant families, it doesn't just matter *what* you are—it doesn't just matter that you're female and forty-eight years old. "It matters that you're Felicity from the FB family, and you're forty-eight years old," Vicki explains. It matters *who* you are.

Felicity knows that this area they've just covered is safe. Her family feels secure at the moment because Felicity's got their back. Often a matriarch will lead from the rear of the group. But when she stops, everyone stops. They're listening to her even when she's behind them. They know right where she is.

A researcher named Lucy Bates collected some urine when a particular elephant in the back of the group she was studying stopped to pee. Then, as the family was moving along, Bates went ahead of them and laid down the urine. When they encountered fresh urine from an elephant they knew was behind them, they seemed truly baffled. They were like, "Wait a minute—how'd she pass us? She's back behind us, but..." This shows, Bates concluded, that elephants are able to hold in mind and regularly update information about the locations of family members.

If something scary happens, the family will rush back to Felicity. If it's dangerous, like a lion or buffalo, she may choose to retreat or have the family charge and drive the intruder off.

"That decision is up to her," Vicki tells me. Right now, Vicki observes, "everyone feels safe and secure, everyone's relaxed; kids are playing. Nobody's worried about anything.

"See, Felicity's an unusually good matriarch. If you have a matriarch who's a suspicious, high-stress type, everybody's always listening for danger." High-stress elephants continually have elevated levels of stress hormones such as cortisol in their blood. That is not good for their metabolism. Vicki says to the elephants, "So it pays to be chilled out, doesn't it, guys?"

Felicity has been leading from the rear but has slowed and dropped even farther behind, as if something is up. Suddenly she wheels, and a hyena peeks out from behind a bush. Felicity stares. She's blown the hyena's cover, so the hyena trots away.

"So—" says Vicki rather proudly. "Felicity is *such* a good matriarch."

They have lives, and they matter to one another. That's really the whole point.

Elephants have wide, layered social networks. Two or more families with special friendliness for each other—special bonds—are called a "bond group."

Adult males live in groups or wander among and between families. Males grow faster than females and continue growing for twice as long.

Babies often rest in the shade while adults stand guard

They can end up twice as heavy. Females reach nearly full body size at around twenty-five years old, eight feet at the shoulder, and can continue bulking to around six thousand pounds. As males continue growing, they can reach eleven to twelve feet at the shoulder; the largest can weigh twelve thousand pounds.

Families may slowly split up if they get too large or if a matriarch dies. On the other hand, small families sometimes join up. Splitting and merging is called "fission-fusion." Because elephants, like humans, live in fission-fusion groups, what they're doing makes sense to us. Social groups of apes, wolves, and certain whales are also fission-fusion.

With elephants, individual personalities matter a lot. They often do things simply because somebody likes somebody else, and they want to hang out. "The fundamental truth of elephants," Vicki sums up, "is that elephants like being with other elephants. They just find it satisfying."

Each elephant in Amboseli probably knows every other adult in the population. But they also know if an elephant is a stranger. In an experiment where recorded calls of elephants they didn't know were played to them, they bunched defensively, raising their trunks, trying to smell the strangers they were hearing.

"When a family is big," Vicki is saying, "it means they have a strong matriarch that everyone likes to follow." Elephants respect their elders with good reason: Survival can depend on an individual with experience and knowledge. In fact, the experience that comes with age matters in everything about elephant society. Elephants are famous for memory because there's a lot to remember.

"So for instance," Vicki relates, "an experienced leader could basically decide, 'We'll be going up those slopes, because I remember there's water there at this time of year, and some grass I know about.'" Elephants sometimes travel hundreds of miles, along routes not used for many years, to arrive at water sources just after the onset of rains. They need to know where they're going. And a lot depends on making the right decisions.

"There's better survival in families with matriarchs older than thirty-five," Vicki explains. Elephants seem to know this. Some families follow *other* families that have older matriarchs.

Elephants have six sets of teeth during their lifetime. The final set appears when they are about thirty years old and can last until they're into their sixties. Eventually their teeth wear down to the gums; when elderly elephants cannot feed properly, they die. And by the time a matriarch dies of natural causes, she usually has mature daughters who themselves have gained sufficient knowledge to competently lead their family. In humans, using knowledge to survive new challenges is sometimes called "wisdom."

However, elder matriarchs' big tusks make them poachers' preferred targets. Elephants are dying younger. Killing elders leaves their family members unprepared. Their matriarch's death triggers, first, devastating psychological consequences. Elephants have extraordinarily close care bonds with their young, and breaking them causes intense suffering. Babies orphaned at under two years of age die soon; orphans under ten die young. Older orphans sometimes wander in bunched-up, leaderless groups. Some families disintegrate. Survivors can carry traumatic memories, making them fearful of and sometimes more aggressive toward humans.

Youngsters learn from elders

CHAPTER 5

Motherhood Happens

"Here's someone feeling a little silly," Vicki says, pointing. "See her with that loose walk and her trunk swaying?"

I do.

"One day when I was new here," Vicki recalls, "the researcher who was orienting me, Norah, and I were watching, and suddenly everyone started running around and trumpeting. I was like, 'What in the world just happened?' Norah said, 'Oh, they're just being silly.'

"I thought, 'Silly?' And the next thing I know, a full-grown female comes along walking on her knees and throwing her head around, acting just daffy. They were just happy. They were like, 'Yaaay!' Everyone says how smart they are. But they can be ridiculous, too. If a young male doesn't have a friend around, sometimes he'll make a little mock charge at us, then back up or twirl around. I actually had one male kneel down right in front of the car and throw zebra bones at me, trying to get me to play with him.

"In wet times, they're happy and jaunty. The rain makes them feel good. I'm just realizing that when I got here, the elephants were still feeling somber from the drought. Now they're coming out of it. You see more nice interactions, or just funny behavior. I'm also seeing how they're being transformed by all these babies. These females seeing their babies tumbling and playing and sleeping; it stimulates a sense of well-being that everything's okay with the family, because, well—babies are great."

Water—and mud—make elephants happy

In motherhood, experience matters. "Females can breed when they're thirteen," Vicki observes, "but a teenage mother is more likely to get into difficulties than a twenty-year-old." Young mothers might go into cold water that chills the baby. They may take their offspring over terrain they can't handle. They might simply not know how to be a mother. When seventeen-year-old Tallulah had her first baby, she acted upset, confused, and generally inept. She didn't have the experience to direct the baby to her nipples and then stand quietly with her leg forward to lower the breast so the little one could suckle. When the baby almost latched its mouth onto a nipple, it promptly got bumped in the nose and knocked over. Then Tallulah did not know how to pry the youngster up. She eventually did figure out what to do.

By contrast, Deborah, who was about forty-seven years old and had given birth several times, was relaxed and competent from the moment her newest baby was born. The baby fell down five times in the first half hour, but Deborah carefully got it up, gently putting a foot under it and steadying it with her trunk. Deborah stood quietly with her leg well forward so her newborn could nurse. Vicki emphasizes, "The older ones are *fantastic* mothers. They're super chill, and by that age they often have loads of helpers."

"They're born knowing how to suckle and follow their mother—that's about all," Vicki says. A newborn elephant can soon walk but otherwise is nearly helpless. In its first week, it can hardly see. For its first months, the baby sticks within range of its mother's touch, often in actual physical contact with its mama. Mother, meanwhile, frequently makes soft, humming sounds to her infant, saying, in effect, "Here I am; I'm right here."

As babies wobble behind, they frequently trip on roots or get trapped in high grass. Adolescent cousins often come to their aid. If a baby falls, all the females run over and make sure it's okay, uttering a special vocalization that helps provide deep reassurance. If the baby gets bullied at all, it makes a squeaky-door cry—*loud*—that brings immediate help. Young females rush so avidly to a baby's aid that they often get in the way of the mother. Experienced mothers then simply let the younger females deal with it.

Aunts and grandmothers are important babysitters, and the experienced mother will be calm as long as she sees to it that her child is with a suitable adult female. Young elephants usually remain within one body length of a family member for the first five years of life.

Newborn getting lifted to his feet for the first time by his twenty-five-year-old mother, Petula (at back, foot raised), and her cousins

Elephants have to *learn* everything about how to be an elephant from other elephants, who protect them.

Babies must also learn trunk management. They often experiment by swinging or tossing or whirling it around, seeing what this thing can do. Sometimes they step on their own trunk and trip. Often they suck their trunk for comfort, the same way a human child sucks its thumb.

I'm watching an eight-month-old trying to pull up some grass. She reminds me of someone learning to use chopsticks; the food won't co-operate. Half the grass falls back to the ground. She looks to her mother, who pulls a sheaf of grass and eats it as if making sure her babe is watching. Often babies reach into the mouths of family members, taking a bit of what they're eating, learning the scents and tastes of vegetation that is good.

"Members of families learn one another's habits," Vicki says. During what part of the day does this family go to drink? Which wetland do they drink at? Those are things they learn as babies from their family. Those things become family traditions.

Now, as a huge unknown male comes swaggering in among several families surrounding us, I see just how *big* males get compared to females. "Wow," Vicki offers, "he's a monster." That female behind him is full-grown and twenty-five years old. He seems twice her size. "Oh, look—she's going over and greeting him." They rumble and briefly wrap trunks. Then he pauses, just standing there with an almost exagger-ated nonchalance, his gigantic trunk draped over a massive tusk. "It's to show females, 'I'm not so scary; look how relaxed and casual I am.' We actually call it 'being casual,'" Vicki tells me.

Meanwhile, Duke, another male who is around fourteen years old, comes to within fifteen feet of me with his trunk extended, sniffing the new human. Just for show, he objects mildly, turning away and then wheeling and sweeping his head up, slapping ears against body and facing us with ears out, then shaking his head haughtily and swinging his trunk impressively. Looking at me with his brown eyes, confronting us so closely with his creased and wrinkled nose-hose and the living leather of his fanning ears, he appears magnificent in every detail and—as far as threatening—not at all convincing.

He could, of course, crush us, but he has no such intention; he's just showing off, as teenage boys often do. He's showing that he's big enough to be taken seriously. But he's not terribly confident. He is trying out his role. He's confident enough in *us* to be focusing some attention on us, yet he isn't threatened by us, isn't really agitated, isn't frightened, doesn't plan to harm us. I know what he's doing. He's expressing, and I'm understanding. He is sending a message, and I'm receiving it. In other words: We're communicating.

Meeting and greeting

Fun in the mud

CHAPTER 6

Playing for Fun

Felicity's tiny baby is about fifty yards away from her mother, up here near us with the rest of the family. She's a particularly confident little elephant. Her big sister is right next to her. Suddenly she runs back to her mother.

"It's a bit of a game," Vicki interprets. "Like, 'Look, I'm over here, and I'm okay!'" She's having fun, ears out, waving her little trunk around, charging an egret. It looks like the *kind* of charge an adult might use to scare off a lion. Part of the family's role is allowing youngsters to explore and learn through their own experiences. Male youngsters tend to play pushing contests against each other. Females tend to play "I'm chasing enemies." Felicity's baby charges a couple more egrets. Even full-sized adults sometimes play games against *imaginary* enemies. They may start running through tall grass, thrashing it, the kind of behavior they might actually use to chase away lions. "But the elephants are playing," declares Vicki. "They know there are no lions."

But—if elephants act like there are lions and there are no lions, isn't it possible they're just making a mistake or being extra careful?

"It's easy to tell," Vicki explains. A serious elephant faced with a real threat pays steady attention. Playing elephants run in a loose and "floppy" way, shaking their heads to let their ears and trunk flap and flop around.

When doing serious things in non-serious moments—staring over their tusks at imagined enemies or shaking their heads before charging and running away in faked fear—playing elephants often seem to be going just for the fun of it. They're all in on the game. Clearly, they're having fun. "Sometimes they put bushes on their heads and just look at you," Vicki says. "Ridiculous."

Fanny's little one flares her ears at us, sizing us up, deciding whether we're now the enemy. She pulls herself up to full height and kind of looks down her nose at us. The little one seems to decide we're either okay or too big to mess with. In a few moments she's under her sister's chin, deciding whether to charge a chicken-like bird called a yellow-necked francolin.

The scene is filled with beautiful innocence. But their lives are not always this perfect. No lives are.

Flanna's ear has a big triangle missing, where a spear went through it. One of these elephants lacks a tail. Hyenas sometimes bite off an elephant's tail while she is giving birth. Hyenas will also seize a baby if they can. Lions can kill smaller elephants. The joys and the dangers are both very real. But these babies must learn all this. They have to be *taught* to fear lions.

CHAPTER 7

Elephant Empathy

All the elephants in view are now busy drinking and feeding. Vicki points to a particular infant nursing from his mother. A few months ago, that infant fell into a well as deep as he is tall.

Vicki went to help rescue him, and his mother was there, upset. "She frantically objected to us using the vehicle to get her away from the well. She almost sat on the fender. But we had to chase her off; it would have been just too terrifying for her to see us roping up her baby. It was all very stressful and very extreme. She stayed nearby, and as soon as we reunited her with her baby, she just suckled him and she wasn't upset with us. I think she understood that we'd intended to help."

Elephants understand cooperation. They aid individuals trapped in muddy riverbanks, helping to retrieve babies, or raising an injured or fallen friend. Once, Cynthia Moss saw a baby elephant fall into a small, steep-sided water hole. The mother elephant and the baby's aunt could not lift the baby out, so the elephants started digging out one side of the hole and made a ramp. They solved their problem, and saved their baby.

Another time, a young mother named Cherie, wanting to rejoin the rest of her family, tried several times to cross a dangerously high-running river in Kenya's Samburu National Reserve. In one disastrous attempt, the waters swept away her three-month-old baby. Cherie pursued her baby through the rough and rapid water, caught up with her, then guided her to calm water on the far bank. The infant must have inhaled a lot of water, though, or perhaps gotten too chilled and gone hypothermic. It reached the shore looking very distressed, and in a little while, it died. In Burma in the mid-1900s, a man named J. H. Williams witnessed an elephant that was swept with her young one into a swollen river: "She pinned the calf with her head and trunk against the rocky bank. Then with a really gigantic effort she picked it up in her trunk and reared up until she was half standing on her hind legs so as to be able to place it on a narrow shelf of rock five feet above the flood level. Having accomplished this, she fell back into the raging torrent and she herself went away like a cork." But half an hour later, as the terrified youngster still shivered in the same spot, Williams heard a mighty roar, "the grandest sounds of a mother's love." Running back along the bank, she retrieved her baby.

Normally, little elephants aren't allowed to get lost. Mothers keep them in sight. No child gets left behind. The matriarch usually paces the herd's travel to make sure the young ones get a chance to rest.

In 1990, here in Amboseli, the famed Echo gave birth to a baby who could not straighten his forelegs, could barely nurse. He shuffled painfully slowly on his wrists, frequently collapsing. Researchers worried that his wrists would be scraped up and get infected. But Echo and her family remained patient. Echo's eight-year-old daughter, Enid, prodded the infant at times, in an attempt to raise him up, but Echo slowly and carefully pushed Enid off, and as they stood over the baby, Enid frequently reached her trunk to Echo's mouth, seeming to seek reassurance.

Elephants often greet each other by touching trunk to mouth, a kind of combined handshake, hug, and kiss

For three days, as the exhausted infant hobbled along, Echo and Enid slowed their pace to his disabilities, continually turning to watch the little one's progress, waiting as he caught up from behind. On the third day, he leaned back until he could put his bent front soles on the ground, then "carefully and ever so slowly," Cynthia Moss wrote, "he transferred his weight back towards the front end of his body and simultaneously straightened all four legs." And though he fell several times, by day four he was walking well and never looked back. His family's persistence—which in humans facing a similar situation we might call faith—had saved him.

"A few days ago," Vicki mentions as we amble along, "Eclipse was suddenly running around, calling, seeming frantic." The family, at that point, was strung out over about 250 yards, with the kids well up ahead with some females. "I think her son was with his friends and just didn't answer her," Vicki speculates. "She was *so* agitated." Then she found him—and everything was fine. Cynthia Moss tells of a one-year-old male who got so absorbed playing with several age-mates from another family that he didn't notice that his own family had moved off. Neither did they realize that they'd left him. Suddenly he panicked and screamed the deep "lost baby" cry. Several females in his family immediately came back for him, and he ran at full speed toward them.

While small babies usually get retrieved quickly, adolescents can become so busy socializing that they get truly separated from their families. "Getting lost like that is *really* scary for them," Vicki tells me. On windy evenings when it's harder for them to hear, she's seen elephants rushing in one direction, calling and then listening, then rushing off in another direction and calling. Reunions can be emotional. "They act like, 'That was the worst thing *everrr*,'" Vicki says, poking fun.

Researchers once saw an elephant pluck up some food and place it into the mouth of another whose trunk was badly injured. "Elephants show empathy," Amboseli researchers Richard Byrne and Lucy Bates state plainly. They aid the ailing. They *help* one another.

More mysteriously, elephants sometimes help people. George Adamson, who helped raise the famous lion Elsa of the book *Born Free*, knew an elderly, half-blind Turkana woman who'd wandered off a path; nightfall caused her to lie down under a tree. She woke in the middle of the night to see an elephant towering over her, sniffing up and down with its trunk. She was paralyzed by fear. Other elephants gathered, and they soon began breaking branches and covering her. The next morning, her faint cries attracted a herder, who released her from the cage of branches. Had the elephants sensed her helplessness and, in empathy and perhaps even compassion, enclosed her in protection from hyenas and leopards? In *Coming of Age with Elephants*, Joyce Poole tells of a herder whose leg was broken in an accidental confrontation with a matriarch. Discovered under a tree along with an aggressive elephant, the herder frantically signaled the search party not to shoot. Later he explained that after striking him, the matriarch had realized that he could not walk and, using her trunk and front feet, had gently moved him a short distance and propped him under the shade of the tree. Occasionally touching him with her trunk, she'd guarded him through the night, though her family left her behind.

Empathy seems quite special. Many believe that empathy "makes us human." Empathy is the ability to match the emotional state of another. Picking up on another's distress or alarm requires your brain to match their emotion. That's empathy. When your companion's fear gets you scared, that's empathy. They yawn and you yawn—empathy.

In play, animals have to know that the individual chasing and attacking them is not serious. Empathy. You have to understand the invitation to play. Empathy. You have to be skilled in the give-and-take of harmless aggression. When you play-bite, you don't bite hard, because of empathy. I see this daily in my dogs Chula and Jude, who play very vigorously with lots of bared teeth and growling but take turns "handicapping" themselves by rolling over or play-crouching, then licking. They're best friends forever, and they know and trust each other. Turns out, many animals are capable of empathy.

We may not know exactly what elephants are feeling, but *they* do. Or perhaps they don't. Perhaps, like us, they simply wonder. I wonder.

Placida, at left, age thirty, with Tee-Jay, twenty-four

CHAPTER 8

Good Grief

Elephants die; we all will. To elephants, as with us humans, it matters who has died. It's why they are "who" animals. The importance of memory, learning, and leadership is why individuals matter. And so, a death matters to the survivors.

A researcher once played a recording of an elephant who had died. The speaker was hidden in some bushes, so the elephants thought they were really hearing the dead elephant calling. The family went wild calling back, looking all around. The dead elephant's daughter called for days afterward. The researchers never again did such a thing.

Elephants' response to death has been called "probably the strangest thing about them." Researcher Joyce Poole has said that when elephants come upon the remains of a dead elephant, "it is their silence that is most unsettling. The only sound is the slow blowing of air out of their trunks as they investigate their dead companion. It's as if even the birds have stopped singing." Vicki has seen it herself; she says it is "heart-stoppingly sad." The elephants cautiously extend their trunks, touching the body gently, as if obtaining information. They run their trunk tips along the lower jaw and the tusks and the teeth: the parts that would have been most familiar in life and most touched during greetings—the most individually recognizable parts.

Cynthia told me of a wonderful matriarch named Big Tuskless. She died of natural causes, and a few weeks later Cynthia brought her jawbone to the research camp to determine her age at death. A few days after that, her family passed through the camp. There were several dozen elephant jaws on the ground in the camp, but the family detoured right to hers. They spent some time with it. They all touched it. And then they all moved on, except one. After the others left, one stayed for a long time, stroking Big Tuskless's jaw with his trunk, fondling it, turning it. He was Butch, Big Tuskless's seven-year-old son. Was he remembering his mother's face, imagining her scent, hearing her voice, thinking about her touch?

Nowadays humans immediately cart off every tusk when an elephant dies. But in 1957, David Sheldrick wrote that elephants have "a strange habit of removing tusks from their dead comrades." He noted "many instances" when elephants carried tusks weighing as much as a hundred pounds up to half a mile away. Iain Douglas-Hamilton described elephants cautiously approaching a dead elephant, drawing nearer with their trunks waving up and down, their ears half-forward. Each seemed reluctant to be first to reach the bones. They advanced in a tight huddle, then began their detailed sniffing and close examination of the tusks. Some bones they rocked and gently rolled with their feet. Others, they clonked together. Some they tasted. Several individuals in turn rolled the skull. Soon all the elephants were investigating. Many carried bones away.

Sometimes they cover dead elephants with soil and vegetation, making them, I think, the only animals besides humans who ever perform burials. When trophy hunters shot a large male elephant, his companions surrounded his carcass. The hunters returned hours later to find that the others had not only covered their dead comrade with soil and leaves but had plastered his large head wound with mud.

Do elephants have a *concept* of death? One day a few years ago, in Kenya's beautiful Samburu National Reserve, a matriarch named Eleanor, ailing, collapsed. Another matriarch, Grace, rapidly approached her with facial glands streaming from emotion. Grace lifted Eleanor back onto her feet. But Eleanor soon collapsed again. Grace appeared very stressed, and continued trying to lift Eleanor. No success. Grace stayed with Eleanor as night fell. During the night, Eleanor died. The next day, an elephant named Maui started rocking Eleanor's body with her foot. During the third day, Eleanor's body was attended by her own family, by another family, and by Eleanor's closest friend, Maya, and again Grace was there. On the fifth day, Maya spent an hour and a half with Eleanor's body. A week after her death, Eleanor's family returned and spent half an hour with her. Recalling this to me, Iain Douglas-Hamilton used the word "grief." After a young elephant dies, the mother sometimes acts depressed for many days, slowly trailing far behind her family.

Do other animals really grieve? In a zoo in Philadelphia in the 1870s lived two inseparable chimpanzees. "After the death of the female," the keeper wrote, "the remaining one made many attempts to rouse her, and when he found this to be impossible his rage and grief were painful to witness.... The ordinary yell of rage ... finally changed to a cry which the keeper of the animals assures me he had never heard before ... *hah-ah-ah-ah-ah*, uttered somewhat under the breath, and with a plaintive sound like a moan.... He cried for the rest of the day. The day following, he sat still most of the time and moaned continuously." More than a century later at the Yerkes Research Center, a chimpanzee named Amos remained in his nest while the others went outside. But the others kept returning indoors to check on Amos. A female named Daisy gently groomed the soft spot behind his ears and stuffed soft bedding behind his back as a nurse might arrange a patient's pillows. Amos died the next day. For days afterward the others acted subdued, eating little. Two male chimpanzees in Uganda had for years been inseparable allies. When one died, the other, who'd been sociable and high-ranking, "just didn't want to be with anybody for several weeks," said researcher John Mitani. "He seemed to go into mourning."

Patricia Wright studies Madagascar's primates, called lemurs (pronounced LEE-murz). Pat says that when a lemur dies, "for the whole family, it's a tragedy." She detailed for me what she observed after a catlike mongoose called a fossa killed a kind of lemur called a sifaka:

"After the fossa left, the family returned. His mate gave the 'lost' call over and over. When sifakas are really *lost*, they give it less often and it's higher and more energetic. But this was a low whistle, mournful, haunting, over and over." Then the dead male's sons and daughters also gave "lost" calls while viewing the corpse from a tree overhead. Over five days, the lemurs returned to the body fourteen times.

Barbara J. King has written, "When two or more animals have shared a life—grief results from love lost." I think that's true for us humans, too.

My wife and I had two ducks, raised together since ducklinghood, who lived with our four chickens. The birds often wandered our yard together, but the ducks were inseparable. They bathed together and, in season, mated. One day, both ducks suddenly fell ill. A day later, the male duck, Duck Ellington, died. Our female, Beeper, recovered. But for days she wandered the yard, the ivy beds, the bushes, calling and searching. Grief? Sorrow? I am not sure how it felt to her, but she clearly missed him and was trying to find him. And eventually she just had to get on with life—as we must. She stopped searching and joined the chickens, becoming the odd duck. As with humans, certain individuals take some losses hard. In 1990, the killer whale matriarch Eve died in the Pacific Ocean off Canada, at age fifty-five. Her sons Top Notch and Foster circled Hanson Island, calling and calling. For the first time in their lives—Top Notch was thirty-three years old—their mother did not return their calls. The two brothers spent days visiting and revisiting the places their mother had been during the last days of her life. Faithfulness, longing. Grief. Daphne Sheldrick, who has half a century's experience with orphan elephants, told me quite matter-of-factly, "An elephant can *die* of grief." She's seen it happen. Daphne says that from her fifty years of raising orphaned elephants, she has learned this: "They grieve and mourn the loss of a loved one, and their capacity for love is humbling."

CHAPTER 9

Elephant Talk

The elephants we're observing move into the marsh, crashing through the tall grass and sloshing into the cooling wetness.

How do families decide where to go, and when? Vicki has watched this *very* carefully. "If someone in the family fancies going to a certain place, she stands at the edge of her group, facing the direction she wishes to travel." It's called a "Let's go" stance. Every minute or so, the elephant with an idea rumbles, "Let's go." It's a proposal: "I want to go this way; let's go together." "Either they agree to go," says Vicki, "or they just won't move."

And if they don't move?

"If they don't move, the one that's wanting to move might come bouncing back to the family and initiate a big greeting to get support. Like, 'Hey! We're really great friends! Now I want to go—*there*.' So a greeting can be a strategy, as well."

Vicki pauses to say, "Hello, Amelia." Then, to me: "That female who's moving and flapping her ears? That's Jolene, the JAs' matriarch.

And—" Vicki looks through her binoculars at a female farther into the marsh and tall grass. "Yeah, okay, so, that's Yvonne."

So: Here we have the AAs, YAs, and JAs. AAs are friends with JAs; YAs are also friends with JAs. They're all going to greet one another. Vicki translates, "They're not just saying, 'Oh, hello.' It's more like, 'This is me and this is you—and we're friends, and we're here.'"

"Want to know whether elephants are good friends or close relatives?" Vicki asks. "Watch their greetings." The more intense and excited the greeting, the more important the relationships. During high social excitement, elephants often suddenly and dramatically grasp one another's trunks, pressing their bodies against each other; there's trumpeting, rumbles, trunks reached toward faces or into another's mouth, ear flapping, tusk clicking.... You can easily see they're excited.

The close one now is Jamila. That next one, who's just put a trunkful of grass on his head, is Jeremy, age nine. If you look just to the right of him, that female whose tusks touch at the tips is Jolene, their current matriarch. Next to her is Jean; she just lost a pregnancy. That female with the very upcurved tusks—that's Jody. Jolene's earned a reputation as a matriarch very sensitive to family needs, calm, quick to offer reassurance, leading by example. "They're a very sweet family with each other, very affectionate. One of my favorite families," Vicki says fondly. Jody is holding her ears out. "That means she's listening," Vicki explains. "And see that small ear flap she just did? They're talking back and forth."

Why can't we hear them?

Elephant song spans ten octaves, from subsonic rumbles to trumpets. Their rumbles, though loud, are often too low-pitched for humans to hear.

Those low rumbles that humans can't hear: Elephants can hear them over distances of several miles through *the ground*. Their great sensitivity to low frequencies comes from their ear structure, bone conduction, and special nerve endings that make their toes, feet, and trunk tip extremely sensitive to vibrations in the ground. In other words, part of elephant vocal communication is received through their feet.

When you do hear an elephant rumbling, you're just catching the top frequency of a vertical wall of sound they're making, like hearing only the higher notes of a complex chord. To put it visually: If the sound were a house, you'd be hearing just the attic of a call that contains a basement.

Elephants create different *kinds* of rumbles. Rumbles during tense encounters sound different from rumbles uttered in peace. Just as humans have different laughs for different contexts and intensities, elephants have different rumbles for different situations.

"A lot of what they're saying is below human hearing," Vicki emphasizes, "but you can see them pause, and you see little postures, subtle little things. You can sometimes see the forehead wrinkle as they call. If you're right next to them, you certainly *can* feel them in your solar plexus, right in your chest; it goes right through you."

What—if anything—*are* they saying?

We can't ask a creature to tell us, but we can observe behavior, ask sensible questions, create some good experiments, and come to a better understanding.

Elephants' interactions show that they understand what they're saying, whether it's specific information, like "Let's go," or more emotional in meaning, such as "I'm getting *impatient*! Let's *go*!" Meaning often depends on context. Because the listener knows the context, they understand the message.

Elephants use well over one hundred ritual gestures to communicate. A shy or nervous elephant may stand listening and watching, twisting the tip of their trunk back and forth; they may touch their own face, mouth, ear, trunk, apparently for reassurance, like a person touching their cheek or putting a hand to their chin.

We've tended to be lazy about other animals' vocabularies. We say merely that dogs "bark" or "whine." That's like saying people "speak" or "cry" and leaving it at that. You can easily hear the difference between your dog barking to be let out and your dog barking at a stranger who has suddenly appeared at the same door. Even to us, the pitch, sound quality, and intensity of what the dog is saying are different, easily recognizable. Your dog understands, and lets you understand.

Yet we remain tone-deaf to other animals' vocabulary. By using a one-size-fits-all word—"bark," "rumble," "howl"—that doesn't actually fit all, we make it unlikely that we will gain an understanding of *their* understanding of what they mean.

Elephants wield a communication kit with dozens and dozens of gestures and sounds and combinations. But for now, they understand what they are saying much better than we do.

African elephants have one particular alarm that appears to be their word for "Bees!" They run from the sound of buzzing bees, shaking their heads as they go.

Baby elephants have two very different "words" that express contentment or annoyance. They respond to being comforted by going *Aauurrrr* and to being insulted—pushed, tusked, kicked, or denied the chance to nurse—by going *Barooo*. Some rumbles by mothers have the immediate effect of bringing a wandering baby back to her side. It seems fair to interpret that as them saying, "Come here."

Vervet monkeys have calls with distinct meanings. In other words: words. If a dangerous cat is detected, the alarm that's given makes everyone run up a tree. When a martial eagle or crowned eagle flies over, the alert monkey's two-syllable call causes the other monkeys to run into thick ground cover (*not* up a tree). A monkey who sees a dangerous snake gives a "chuttering" call that causes other vervets to stand up on their hind legs, scanning the ground for the reptile.

Two elephants approaching each other give a soft, short greeting rumble. When human caretakers call an orphaned elephant's name, the one they've called often replies with this same greeting rumble. (In effect, the caretaker speaks English and the elephant replies in elephant.) Researchers say it means something like, "Hello, it's good to be near you again" or, perhaps, "You are important to me."

After eating, the elephants gather closely, adults facing out, children in the middle. Jean is very slowly backing into Jolene, touching her. "See them all standing together now, leaning against each other, touching with tails, trunks—. This is perfect. Everyone's feeling really safe. They'll probably have a snooze now."

Babies sprawl abundantly, dozing peacefully within their tribe's safekeeping. The adults just stand quietly. At least it seems quiet.

"All that ear flapping?" says Vicki. "They're talking." We can't hear them.

CHAPTER 10

It's Going to Be Tough

In camp this morning, a new report is circulating, telling us that in the last ten years, poachers have killed *one hundred thousand* African elephants. That in the last ten years, central Africa has lost about 65 percent of its elephants, and they are dwindling everywhere.

The numbers numb me. The difference between that cruelty and these kind creatures with whom I have fallen in love shatters my ability to think.

They are being killed just for their tusks, which are made into ivory carvings such as little statues, bracelets—it's an incredible waste of these beautiful lives.

This park's border is open—elephants walk in and out. Amboseli elephants leave, Kilimanjaro elephants arrive, they all wander into Tanzania and back. So if there's such risk to them, why not just fence elephants in and people out?

"That's not nature conservation," Vicki asserts defiantly. "And we don't even know whether fenced parks can work long-term any more than can a zoo. We can't afford to lose more habitat; we've lost too much already."

One Amboseli male went to Lake Natron, about eighty-five straight-line miles from here. These are real elephants, in other words. They live the way the world made them, the way they are made for the world.

This elephant's trunk shows a newly healed spear wound. When the local Maasai people are herding their cattle, they sometimes try to push elephants away from water holes. Sometimes elephants push them. Sometimes a spear gets thrown. The mere thought is too painful.

"Looks better," Vicki assesses. It had been leaking fluid.

"Elephants sometimes kill people," Vicki reminds me. "Some elephants just *hate* people and will take any opportunity to hurt them."

I ask why.

"Something bad happened. I can't imagine that an elephant who hasn't had a negative interaction with humans would hate humans."

What proportion of the elephants here have experienced or seen human violence toward elephants?

"Hmm…" Vicki thinks about this. "Every member of the AAs over ten years old has experienced losing a family member to humans. And the AAs don't even really leave the park. The JAs also don't leave the park, but that big hole in Jackson's ear is from a spear. EBs, EAs… Y'know, now that I think of it, every single family has experienced something negative and violent with humans."

That means they've witnessed an attack by people and have been involved in the panic. Some have felt the pain of injury.

Later in the day we encounter a large herd of elephants commuting up out of the marsh for the night, marching across plains lit in gold-slanted sunlight. As we sense and can plainly see, their major self-governing principle is simply "Live and let live." The elephants' way is humbler than ours. They demand less of the world. They take less from the world. They live in better harmony with the rest of their world.

While hundreds of other elephants plod across the dusty plains toward distant hills, one family, for whatever reason, is still blowing water and rolling in a deep, lushly vegetated spring-fed pool. Maybe they're just having too much fun.

They submerge like hippos and spout like whales; they roll and splash and plow underwater with only their rumps showing. They periscope their trunks, snorkeling the air, moving along like black submarines.

After a while, they move single file to a farther bank and emerge shiny and wet like autos from a carwash. But one has not yet even gone in. She remains on the bank with her baby. Her baby is hesitant. The mother is patient. She is touching the water with her trunk but is waiting. Eventually the mother enters. The baby follows. The baby gets alongside her mother and wraps her trunk around her mother's tusk for support. Soon the water floats the baby, and the mother, with her trunk, guides her child along.

An enormous male named Tim

Elephants stream emotion from glands on their cheeks, and show it with a raised tail

CHAPTER 11

Ivory

"I cannot tell them, 'This man is writing a book; be nice to him,'" Julius Shivegha is saying. "They will see you as a good person if you are a good person."

The youngest of the elephants he is standing among reaches his tiny trunk up to Julius's mouth. Normally, a baby puts its trunk to its mother's mouth to learn, from food she is chewing, the scent of safe and nourishing plants. This query—"What are you eating?"—later becomes the elephants' trunk-to-mouth greeting, perhaps a bit similar to humans' kissing. Julius takes the little trunk, blowing into it playfully.

This baby was two weeks old when found alongside his fatally wounded mother. And there is one marked by a machete. And there is Quanza, sole survivor of a famously photographed Amboseli family. Because she was more than a year old at the time of the attack, Quanza's mind recorded an imprint of terror and confusion. "She is still very agitated," Julius says. "If they are mourning or grieving, you see that."

Made orphans by the illegal killing of elephants for their ivory tusks, these luckier few young ones have been rescued and brought here to the David Sheldrick Wildlife Trust, in Nairobi.

In many places in the last few centuries, humans have hunted elephants completely out of existence. Elephants were gone from much of China literally before the year 1 and from much of Africa by the year 1000. Since Roman times, humans have reduced Africa's elephant population by perhaps 99 percent.

Elephants' main message in a bottle: vulnerability. Ivory is elephant tusks carved into statues and bracelets and other things. Ivory has been in demand for thousands of years. Ivory would not be a problem if people just waited for elephants to die naturally. But for thousands of years, humans have killed elephants for their tusks. And demand for ivory continues, more so than ever. Almost no place is truly safe for an elephant.

Three hundred miles north of Amboseli is the great and beautiful landscape of Samburu National Reserve. Samburu, like Amboseli, is one of the few remaining places where elephants can live without being in constant fear of humans. But the fear is here, too.

Shifra Goldenberg downshifts to neutral, and as our dust clears she explains that an elephant named Wendy is not here with the rest of her family. Her four-year-old—also not here.

Wendy has previously been shot. Her two youngsters were shot. The wildlife veterinarian tranquilized and treated them. Wendy and one youngster recovered. Wendy is wearing a collar for pinpointing her location. Two days ago, Wendy led her whole family about fifteen miles to Shaba National "Reserve." "Reserve" is in quotes because Shaba has become dangerous for elephants. Now Wendy's family is back here without Wendy, and they seem upset.

Shifra calls Gilbert Sabinga at our Samburu camp. He tells us he'll try to access Wendy's collar signal. We wait. Shifra is a graduate student studying the effects of poaching on the social lives of elephant families. Gilbert works for a conservation group called Save the Elephants.

Collars tell of travels invisible. One male went 155 miles (250 kilometers) in four days, mainly through farmland, traveling only at night and hiding by day. He knew well, it seems, that he was transiting dangerous territory.

Gilbert finally calls back. There's a problem. Wendy's collar's scheduled nine a.m. report never came. The other collars all reported their signals.

David Daballen and Lucy King arrive. David is field manager for Save the Elephants. Lucy works to reduce villager-elephant conflict.

Now on his cell phone, David is being informed that at the wetlands about fifteen miles away, two gunmen were firing shots at a group of elephants in an attempt to herd them out of the water to a spot where they could be slaughtered. The elephants panicked, and village women in their farm plots, seeing the stampeding elephants, began screaming. What I am gathering in the commotion of David trying simultaneously to listen and to convey the situation is that the elephants fled north, toward here.

David Daballen of Save the Elephants

David and Lucy decide to continue farther along the riverbank while Shifra and I stay put.

A few minutes later, Shifra's phone goes off.

It's Lucy. They've found Wendy where a small stream—the Isiolo River—enters the Ewaso Ng'iro, the main river, inside the Buffalo Springs National Reserve. She's fine.

I can almost hear all our bodies relax with relief. By the time we join David and Lucy, Wendy's collar is again reporting, and Lucy has displayed her travels on a computer. Last night, Wendy's group suddenly came straight back here from the wetlands, with no rest. It's called "streaking." Lucy shows us the map, narrating: "See them moving outside the reserve. This marsh here is very lush, so they like it; that's where they've been. And now look here between midnight and three a.m.; they're skirting the village. This is dangerous territory." There are human dwellings, farms....

"The hot zone for poaching," offers David.

"Look at them streaking in the dark, absolutely hoofing it."

Now, on the riverbank, we watch for two hours as Wendy's dozing family scarcely moves a muscle. They must be exhausted after last night's stressful foray for food. Eventually they stroll into the river, drink, cross, and disappear up the opposite bank.

This morning in trees over the camp, monkeys are busy with urgent things while we enjoy breakfast.

David's phone rings and he rises to his feet to answer it, walking from the table as he talks. Quickly he returns, announcing, "Another elephant, right off the road across the river, just discovered killed.

"This is the worst it's ever been," David mutters.

David and I wade across the river. I'm worried about the crocodiles. "They don't attack adults here," David reassures me. "Only sometimes kids."

Ivory trade is about poor people who need money and greedy people who already have plenty. Behind much of it are criminals and corrupt government officials who exploit poor people and elephants both. So ivory is not just about elephants. It would be far simpler if it were.

Of course, ivory is also about elephants. Elephants that are intelligent and sensitive and social and live with their families and need their mothers. From an estimated ten million elephants in the early 1900s, they're down to less than half that. During the ivory crisis of the 1980s,

Cynthia Moss estimated that 80,000 elephants were going into the ivory grinder annually. Tanzania lost a staggering 236,000 elephants during those years. Sierra Leone saw its final elephants killed in 2009. Many other countries in Africa lost 80 to 90 percent of their elephants.

All of this robs elephants, of course, but it takes from people, too. In Kenya alone, 300,000 people rely directly on tourism for employment, and every tourist comes wanting to see elephants.

A hundred years ago, Europeans and Americans were the main ivory buyers, and now Chinese culture has moved in. Currently in Africa, an estimated 30,000 to 40,000 elephants are being killed illegally every year. Today Africa's elephant population is about one hundred fewer than yesterday's. About every fifteen minutes, another gets killed.

Like the one we're headed to.

Vultures flag the huge gray corpse. David and I walk from the dusty road and approach. It's Philo.

Philo was a young male, fifteen years old, only halfway to being a viable contender for breeding. From just below his eyes, Philo's face is entirely mutilated. His miraculous trunk lies a few yards away, like a discarded rubber pipe. His tusks, gone.

"They take the tusks and leave four tons rotting. Such a stupid thing." David quietly smolders with a pressurized anger that runs like molten lava beneath his hard-baked crust.

Working backward along Philo's tracks, David determines that he was hit right over there on that rise, ran bleeding two hundred yards to here, then collapsed. After he collapsed, they shot him several times in the back of the head. Like an execution. One of those bullet holes is still bubbling crimson blood.

Four days ago, visiting researcher Ike Leonard captured Philo's last portrait. The photo shows Philo as a promising young bull jauntily showing off a bit of teenage swagger. Ike is an elephant keeper with Disney's Animal Kingdom. He had come to see how he might improve the welfare of the captive elephants he cares for in Orlando, Florida. He wanted to observe, he'd told me, "how wild elephants live." We are also observing how elephants die.

If you ever see a lovely ivory carving, think about the elephant that was killed to make it. No one should buy ivory. Every time someone buys an ivory carving, it gives someone a reason to kill *another* elephant.

David, Shifra, and I are at the river before sunset. As if miraculously, group after group of elephants caravan out of the trees and cross the river toward us. Mothers, babies, elephants of all ages.

Up and down the river, lines of elephants are crossing, sloshing easily through the slow-flowing sheet of brick-red water. The numbers build to a count of around 250 elephants drinking and socializing. Elephants doing elephant things is an indication that a lot of good remains.

David switches the ignition off, thinking there'll be no engine noise to bother the oncoming families. But they turn around, bunch up, and raise their trunks, sniffing suspiciously. Voices without an engine are frightening to them now. Tourists are safe and have idling engines. Poachers don't have engines. David restarts the engine, and they relax.

Refreshing and relaxing

CHAPTER 12

They Know Who They Are

A fresh wind blows the clouds from the slopes of Kilimanjaro on a new Amboseli morning, leaving the mountain's nineteen-thousand-foot-high snows seeming to float above its blue shoulders.

Katito and I are with Felicity's family. "Such a nice family," Katito says. "I'm glad you got to meet them."

At ten-thirty in the morning, they pour themselves back into the marsh. Into one pool they submerge and roll. A big male named Wayne hoses himself repeatedly with muddy water. Babies are kicking the water just to watch their own big splashes, having so much fun that they seem to be smiling. Lubricated by the thick mud, they're squiggling over one another, rejoicing in so fine a bath, squirming upon the muddy banks and rolling back into the pileup.

Many, many other families are easing themselves into the cooling waters of the marsh. In the last hour, a breathtaking four hundred elephants have flowed past us in two great waves. We maneuver to the top of a hill. For long minutes we watch hundreds of elephants living their lives. Eating, nursing, growing. The babes climbing playfully over one another. Males testing their status. Females keeping a watchful eye—and ear, and trunk.

Katito's gentle voice suddenly breaks into the heat, almost whispering: "I was there when Echo died." Echo, the wise and powerful matriarch who Cynthia had learned so much from. Katito's voice comes so soft on the dry breeze it actually seems to deepen the silence. "I was the one holding her head. May 5th, 2009, two-thirty p.m.

Katito Sayialel can identify nine hundred individual elephants on sight

"One morning I saw Echo with two daughters, one nine years old, one four. Echo was dragging herself like an old grandmother. I just shook my head. The drought was very bad. And Echo was no longer young. She was sixty-four, you know. Next morning, six-thirty, I got called: 'The elephant with the crossed tusks...' I rushed there. Echo had collapsed. I'll show you the spot. She was lying on the ground, kicking, opening her eyes, trying to raise herself. People came with a truck and a rope. They said, 'We'll put the rope under her and try to pull her up.' I said, 'No.' I knew she was dying. Natural death. Caused by drought. I said, 'We will just stay, and watch her.' Two of Echo's daughters were there. They didn't even chase us.

"We stayed all night, all the next morning, into the afternoon. People brought food. I was holding Echo's head. Just soothing her, cooling her. Her daughter Enid didn't even move. She was there until her death, like mourning all the time.

"I had my arms around Echo's head and then, she just stretched her leg out very slowly. And she blinked her eye and looked at me. It was so sad to me when I saw that. And then her eye closed. And she died.

"Echo's daughter Enid was really hit by her death. Oh, yes. Her sad face; I cannot describe it. Like a human being who has lost a family member and has been crying. That is how her face looked, for a month. Quite a long time. She lost weight.

"Echo's sister Ella had gone to Tanzania for a few weeks. Ella and Echo had never gotten along very well. Ella is very independent-minded. I can say, Ella is mean. Some elephants, you can say they have a good heart, a cool head; they're nice. Ella is mean.

"When Ella returned, she realized Echo was dead.

"Ella is the oldest now, forty-one. She is acting as though she is the matriarch, but she is not behaving like a matriarch should. Eudora is forty years old now, but—she cannot be a leader. She doesn't know how. Eudora is flaky. No one follows her.

"The one who is behaving like a true matriarch is Echo's daughter Enid. Echo had been training Enid to take over. Enid is leading the family, even though she is only thirty. Enid is not timid, so if something happens and they are scared, they all bunch to Enid. They feel she will be able to protect them."

Echo's family did extremely well under her leadership, growing from just seven members in 1974 to more than forty at the time of her death. By any measure, she had an exceptional reign.

Now Enid makes the decisions. Enid has taken the family away, something Echo never did. In fact, they've been gone nearly three months. "We're worried that Enid might have taken them to Tanzania," Katito says. "When she comes back, we'll see whether they've lost anybody."

Late afternoon. We'd gone back to camp to get Vicki, and now we're out again.

"You hear that rumble?" Katito suddenly comes to attention. "Calling the family."

I hear it, but also the air vibrates and I feel it, too. I see that many of the elephants are rallying their families together. Within the vast herd, the family groupings are now becoming much more apparent as the individuals gather with whom they need to, preparing to move upland in families, the families gathered into bond groups. So *interesting* to watch happening.

The astonishing gathering of four hundred elephants is beginning to march in waves from the downtown marsh to the bedroom hills.

I watch two little ones chasing each other, one trying to bite the other's tail and jumping up to put its forelegs briefly on its playmate's back as they walk along. The mood is fun.

What their lifetime holds in the coming days and decades, no one can say.

I feel sure I will never again see so many elephants in one place. They are right here, and we are elephant-wealthy beyond measure. I miss them already.

A family on the move

INTERLUDE:

BETWEEN LAND
AND WATER

As I mentioned at the outset of our journeys, this book is about the biggest animals on land and in the ocean. So from elephants we're now going to—whales. Specifically, we are about to get familiar with the sea's most awesome dolphin: the orca, or killer whale.

What do elephants and orcas have in common? Well, they're big. They're both air breathers, like us. And like us they're mammals. As mammals we all have a lot in common. Mammals make milk; no other animals do that. We have the same skeleton. Even the hands and feet of humans, elephant feet, and whale flippers all have the same bones; they're just arranged and shaped a little differently. The finger bones in a whale flipper are like a hand in a mitten. And basically we have the same organs, the same nervous system, the same hormones that create mood and motivation. Plus, like elephants, killer whales have big, big brains and are very smart.

From the outside we look different. But the similarities between a whale and an elephant are greater than the differences. You could think of it this way: An elephant is a mammal outfitted for hiking, a whale is outfitted for diving. It's a little like how a human in backpacking gear looks different on the outside from a person snorkeling with a dive mask and fins. But under the gear, there's a lot in common. And under their exterior, elephants and orcas have lots in common with each other. And with us. Under the skin, we are all kin.

So welcome aboard. Let's head to the sea.

PART TWO

Killer Whales

*Exception might be taken to the name bestowed upon this whale . . .
for we are all killers.*

—Herman Melville, *Moby-Dick*

A resident orca surfaces with a salmon in the waters off Washington state

CHAPTER 13

Sea Rex

Ken Balcomb lives in a house perched among pines on a slope with a wide and wondrous view from San Juan Island across Haro Strait.

Today the water is rough, whitecaps and foam, and the wind is spitting rain, and gulls are shooting by on near-gale gusts. Across the strait, Vancouver Island, Canada, appears as mountains beyond blue mountains between blue sky and blue water. In the strait live the world's largest constellation of sea stars, the planet's most far-reaching octopus—and the world's largest dolphins: killer whales. Some people prefer to call them orcas. Whatever you call them, they own this place. Shore to shore and surface to seafloor, the whales know it as their country.

In no other living room have I ever felt so much like I was in a museum. On a low coffee table rests a skull three and a half feet long, weighing 150 pounds. Its enormousness and those rows of interlocking teeth make it the closest thing to *T. rex*. It's Sea rex. And it lives.

Somewhere out there right now swim creatures wielding skulls like this one, taking their living by these massive jaws and those rows of thumb-thick daggers: intelligent, maternal, long-lived, cooperative, intensely social, devoted to family—. They are, like us, warm-blooded milk-makers, mammals whose personalities are really not much different from ours. They're just a lot bigger. And notably less violent. The brains—also a lot bigger—manage the tasks of family, geography, social networking, and the detailed analysis of sound.

Ken has just started explaining how the whales use sonar when, for some reason, my gaze shifts past the windows, to the moving water in the strait.

Just beyond the near-shore kelp bed, my eye catches a sudden puff of vapor. But no fin. I can't imagine that a killer whale could breathe without showing its high-flying dorsal fin, but at that moment the sea slits open and out bursts a starkly black-and-white head.

Whoa! But why didn't it announce itself? The speakers on Ken's kitchen windowsill continually stream sound from a nearby array of underwater microphones called hydrophones, via OrcaSound.net. So far, the speakers have been quiet.

Hurrying to the big, tripod-mounted binoculars at his kitchen windows, Ken scans. "Could be transients," he says intently. "They're usually silent."

There are a couple of fins now.

"Not traveling fast, just looking around…" He scrutinizes the scene, then adds, "Fairly broad-based fin on that male. Long dive time. More and more like transients."

Transients: mammal eaters. The "resident" killer whales are fish eaters who mainly chase salmon; they're usually chatterboxes, very vocal. The transients can be quiet stalkers, cloaked in silence from the seals, dolphins, sea lions, and occasional whales they seek—for whose breaths and bubbles they listen.

Minutes pass with no sight of blow or fin. I ask, "How could they just—disappear?"

"Oh, transients can do that. Soft blows, like that first puff you saw. Not putting a fin up, long dives—. Many a careful watcher has gotten the slip from transients." Fully a quarter of an hour later, there they are again, off the point.

"Oh—" breathes Ken, his eyeballs buried in the binoculars. "That's, I think, T-19."

An identification seems impossible in the rough sea.

"See the fin leaning slightly toward the left?"

T, for Transient. Constantly, they move. Abruptly they can disappear. Suddenly here they are.

There's another male with a more erect fin. And another, possibly a young male. Coming on slowly. Close to shore. Farther off, two females.

"Oh yeah, yeah, yeah," Ken says, his eyes glued to his binocular lenses. "Oh boy."

Well ahead of the males, a harbor seal pops its head up. Looks

Members of L pod traveling together

around. The males are moving with deceptive speed. And the seal is, one might say, dead ahead.

"The seal hasn't—" Ken starts. "Reaction is crucial, but—"

The seal slips from the surface like a raindrop. Visibility underwater here is only about ten feet. The seal is about a hundred yards from the nearest whale. Its problem: timing. To sonar-wielding whales, the seal might as well be a black silhouette on a light table.

Suddenly the three nearby males are surging through a spreading patch of slick water.

"Well, that seal should have acted immediately," says Ken.

One of the whales lunges through the surface, jaws clenching part of the seal.

They've shared it. These males are twenty-six to twenty-eight feet long and weigh about seventeen thousand pounds. The seal they've just torn to pieces probably weighed about as much as a large person. Yet mysteriously, no free-living killer whale has ever killed a human.

Seal-hunting killer whales need about a seal a day each, roughly 250 pounds. They'll chase, catch, and consume seals several times a day, sharing them. Even a resident orca who catches a salmon that could be swallowed in one gulp almost always shares it with family members.

People uncomfortable with the word "killer" have long since called these whales "orcas" after their Latin name, *Orcinus orca.* But the word "orca" itself refers to a sea monster; it's not very flattering, either.

Researchers usually call them simply "killer whales." They're the world's largest dolphins and they're the baddest whales out there. They're the sea creature that nothing in the sea dares to hunt.

In under five minutes, Ken has downloaded his photos and is confirming IDs. "That was T-19, T-19b, T-19c, T-20...." T-20 is about fifty years old. Ken clicks through the pages of these whales' photos and genealogies. Births. Deaths. Family relationships.

Mysteries, too. No one had ever seen the T-20 group before 1984; now they show up annually. One whale, T-61, vanished for thirteen years—then returned.

Ken is explaining how killer whales are masters at the production and analysis of sound. Even in a world of cold, green, murky water, they generate sound to unveil prey far beyond visibility. Sonar and their other calls also help them stay in touch with their comrades and children dozens of miles away.

Ken explains some differences between the mammal-eating transients and the fish-eating residents. Residents form stable groups of families called "pods." Transient groups split and merge. Transients hunt in small, quiet groups. Residents sometimes form chatty, playful multi-pod crowds. Transients often hold their breath for fifteen minutes. Resident whales seldom stay down more than five. Pretty big differences.

When mammal-eating transients hear the fish-eating residents' cheerful chirps a few miles away, they detour or even turn around. You might guess that the mammal eaters are fiercer—they do pack more robust jaw muscles—but residents usually move in larger groups.

All in all it's been a typical Sunday at Ken Balcomb's home, where Ken has spent most of his life on the lookout for "killer" whales. Never mind what they're called. He knows them better than just about anybody.

CHAPTER 14

A Complex Species

For a long time, humans believed one species of killer whale roamed worldwide, in groups led by males, and ferocious enough to kill any whale—and certainly any human—that swam within its furious clench. Wrong. Decades of watching, listening, tagging, and genetic sleuthing have pulled the veil off not just a new killer whale but *numerous* new killer whales.

Turns out, several "types" of killer whales swim the North Pacific. We've already met "transients," who travel widely. "Residents" stay closer to the coast during summer and fall, looking for salmon that are funneling toward coastal streams for spawning. The rest of the year, they're gone from here.

But transients' and residents' *diets* (not their travels) distinguish them. Transients show no interest in fish as they pursue mammals. Residents have no interest in eating mammals. So we have transients and residents and—. Out in the North Pacific roam little-known "off-shores," whose existence wasn't even suspected until 1988, when researchers puzzled over smaller whales, with different calls, who were hunting sharks.

No one's ever seen the different types mingling. DNA shows that North Pacific fish-catching (resident) and mammal-hunting (transient) killer whales have avoided interbreeding for about half a million years.

At present, scientists know of eight or so various "types"— including Antarctic types A, B, and C, pack-ice killer whales, and others. Their main differences are in what they eat. And they're surprisingly picky eaters. One Antarctic orca type prefers a certain kind of seal called the Weddell seal. One mainly hunts fish called toothfish (sold as "Chilean seabass," they can weigh two hundred pounds). One type specializes in catching penguins.

Because the types don't mix and don't interbreed, they fit the definition of separate species. It's likely that scientists will eventually recognize and name them as such. That means some of the largest species on Earth are yet to be fully "discovered." Amazing.

We humans talk through our mouths. Dolphins, including orcas, are different. A dolphin forces air through the nasal passages inside their head, then—this is weird—they process and amplify the vibrations through a special rounded fatty "acoustic lens" in their forehead (this, not their skull, gives dolphins their rounded, "melon-headed" shape). The energy exits the dolphin's head as a beam of sound.

Their hearing is even odder. Incoming vibrations striking their lower jaw get picked up by oil in hollow jawbones and carried to their inner ears. I guess you could say their jawbones perform the sound-collecting function of the outer ears of other mammals, though very differently.

The sonar-using "toothed whales"—the dolphins (including, of course, killer whales), porpoises, pilot whales, belugas, and sperm whales—have more than triple the number of nerve fibers in their ears as do land mammals. Their massive hearing nerves are the largest-diameter nerves in any creature of any kind. Why so many and so big? For sending and receiving large quantities of information in the form of sound, at very high speeds.

After dinner, before bed, laptops closed, we're sitting in Ken's kitchen just chatting, when through the little speakers comes a single whistle that stops all conversation.

The quiet nighttime fills with squeaks, chatters, whoops, buzzes, whistles, whines, and squeals. Resident orcas! It sounds as if, on an empty, dark road, a Dixieland band has just come round a distant bend. Coming nearer, getting louder.

For twenty minutes, from out in the darkness, they parade past us, whistling and chirping like rain-forest birds, sounding confident and energetic. Their sound builds and peaks. And then the sound begins fading.

It's the superpod! Here they come. Awesome!

CHAPTER 15

Super Social

In the morning, Ken comes downstairs announcing, "We have whales!" Their sounds again begin coming through the windowsill speakers. Whines, whistles, whoops—.

Who is it?

Ken holds up a finger to pause me. "Oh—there's a K; hear that kind of mewey, meek-sounding call, like little kittens? Uh; there's more than one pod there right now. I'll know better in a moment." Pause. "There's J pod," Ken offers. "J- and L-pod calls are more like honks and horns." Pause. "Okay; I hear Js, Ks, *and* Ls—all three pods!"

We step onto Ken's kitchen deck. Sure enough, rounding the point a mile to our south, lined up in a broad front, killer whales come bursting energetically through steep whitecaps. This is a big bunch of whales; from left to right they span my binoculars' entire field of view and then some, even at this distance. "Wow—there might be sixty, seventy-five whales out here!"

"They might *all* be here," Ken says, excited.

Indeed, *all* the killer whales of all three "resident" pods that are ever seen in these waters—J, K, and L pods—are headed our way. It's "a superpod!" Ken exclaims.

During superpod aggregations, "the real old and real young ones like hanging out with each other," Ken narrates. "Females who haven't seen each other for months just stay together for days on end, and chat around as if wanting to talk about what they did all winter. The young like rolling and tumbling and chasing one another."

There's no other creature on Earth with a society quite like that of these fish-eating resident killer whales of the Pacific Northwest. As with elephants, the basic social unit is a family led by a senior female matriarch, with her children and her daughters' children. The big difference: Although young male elephants leave their family as they mature, male killer whales stay in their birth family for their entire life. (They mate when socializing with other families but are soon back at their mama's side.) Mother-child bonds remain extremely strong, lifelong. And, in fact, in no other known creature do all children— daughters *and* sons—stay with their mother for the rest of her life.

As with elephants, each killer whale family's matriarch has memorized the family's survival manual: the knowledge of the region, the routes and island passes, the rivers where salmon concentrate in their seasons, and so on. She's often out in front. They swim seventy-five miles a day, commanding large areas.

Families who share a small number of calls that are not used by other families are called a "pod." No pod uses all the same calls of another pod. Families within a pod tend to socialize together a lot. So a killer whale pod is several families who regularly socialize. It's a lot like an elephant bond group.

Pods who socialize at least occasionally are called a "community." Communities *don't* socialize with other communities, even though they are the same type of orca. Here in the Northwest, the two separate communities are the northern residents and the southern residents. There are eighty-some southern resident whales. The northern residents total about 260.

These two communities avoid mixing for what appear to be purely *cultural* reasons. Northern and southern residents have been seen feeding less than a thousand yards apart—but never mingling. The DNA shows these non-mingling neighbors as genetically the same species. Yet one definition of *different* species is "two populations that do not freely interbreed."

So, we could be seeing killer whales openly in the process of separating into different species. If they continue to avoid each other, these different communities could eventually evolve into different species. (Check back in a hundred thousand years.) This self-segregation is so unusual that, researchers say, it has "no parallel outside humans."

Researchers have long been impressed by the lack of fighting among killer whales. Alexandra Morton writes of the synchronized breathing among family members, the way all the whales continually touch one another as they swim along, lightly running their flippers along the flanks of their companions or indulging in full-body contact;

of the way no killer whale seems subordinate or second-class. She writes of the close interactions between mothers and children. She is impressed by killer whales' "acceptance, approval, and peace."

The superpod of partying whales is headed in our direction. Blasting along in high gear, they stage an impressive show.

One male turns around with his head out, as if looking to see how many of his companions are up. A few more rise, bunched closely, cutting the water with the tall slice of those awesome dorsals. Underwater, they're catching fish. A few gulls streak to the surface, grabbing floating fish scraps. Success in fishing seems to have the whales in a lighthearted mood, splashing and socializing and looking relaxed.

Do they talk to each other and tell stories? We don't know. What they're thinking: We don't know. What they're saying: We don't know. Can we begin to know?

Like human babies, infant dolphins babble sequences of whistles that become more organized as they grow. At anywhere between one month and two years, bottlenose, Atlantic spotted, and other dolphins develop their own distinctive individual "signature whistles." Signature whistles are a name they create for themselves. The sound is distinctive, and the dolphin doesn't change it, ever. They use it to announce themselves.

Dolphins who hear their own signature whistled by another dolphin call back. In other words, they call each other by name, and they answer when they hear their own name called. Dolphins call their close friends' names when they are separated. No other mammal except humans seems to do that (that we know of). Dolphins more than ten miles away can often hear each other. Atlantic spotted dolphins seemingly use names to call together several individuals. When groups meet at sea, they exchange names.

Researchers have recently realized that various bat species, too, sing songs that include individualized names for themselves. Some researchers think that all 350-plus parrot species probably use signature calls. In "an intriguing parallel with human parents naming infants," say researchers, green-rumped parrotlet parents name their young ones, who then use those given names to refer to themselves. And Australian superb fairy wrens teach their unhatched chicks a password, and "the better they learn the password, the more they will be fed." Surely, in the enormous gap between dolphins and fairy wrens, there must be much, much more that we are so far missing, things currently unheard of.

Of course, dogs and others easily recognize their given names. Our smart little Chula knows who to run and find when I say, "Go get Jude" (her adopted brother) or "Go get Mommy" (her lady caregiver—my wife). And they understand "water" and "toy." And, certainly, "treat."

When captive bottlenose dolphins heard recorded signature whistles of dolphins with whom they'd been housed as long as twenty years earlier, they remembered and responded. The experimenter concluded, "Dolphins have the potential for lifelong memory for each other." It was the first experiment proving that a non-human could remember another individual for decades.

But more informally, apes and elephants and some other species have, after separations of many years, reunited very touchingly with lost companions or human caregivers. Several such heart-rending re-unions, caught on video, can be viewed on the Web.

What else is going on in the world's biggest brains?

CHAPTER 16

Singing and Sonar

Some people have put a lot of time into listening to whales. In the 1970s, scientists realized that humpback whales sing structured songs. Strangely, even if they're coming from thousands of miles apart, males converging on mating grounds all sing the same song. The song lasts about ten minutes. Then the whale repeats it. They sing for hours. Each ocean's song is different. Over months and years it changes in the same way for all the thousands of whales in each ocean.

Killer whales of one family can be spread out over 150 square miles—and all be in vocal contact. Through the hydrophones I've been hearing their chirps, whistles, honks, whoops, and whatever you'd call what sounds like wet hands on a latex balloon. Most of the calls have sudden shifts or sweeps in pitch.

"A call might sound like *Ee-rah'i, ee-rah'i*," says Ken. "Does that mean something specific? Or does its *intensity* carry meaning? When the pods congregate, you sense intensity, excitement; it *sounds* like a party. When they're excited, the calls get higher and shorter—in other words, shrill."

They don't seem to have one call for "prey" and another for "hello." Ken feels certain, however, that "*they* know—from just a peep—who that was and what it's about. And that their voices are as different and recognizable as our voices are to us." *Pituuu* is a call that kind of means, "We're doing this now; let's keep doing this together"; *Wee-oo-uuo* is a call of tranquility and relaxed contact ("How we doing—good? Good").

I ask if we're hearing the sonar they use to find fish.

"No. Sonar sounds like—" Ken rapidly clicks his tongue. "Sometimes they come on the speakers with those clicks; that's them 'looking' for fish."

Clicks return an echo that the brain can use to extract information. Dolphins using sonar can detect a ping-pong ball one hundred yards away, a distance at which many humans would fail to see it. They can track rapidly swimming fish well enough to capture them, meanwhile avoiding obstacles while traveling at high speeds. They click fast: Each click lasts just ten millionths of a second, and they make up to four hundred clicks per *second.*

So much of a dolphin's head hardware and brain wiring is devoted to production and analysis of underwater sound, it's as if each individual functions as a sophisticated undersea spying station. Whales likely hear their friends and families' social voices quite similarly to the way we hear ours. After all, it's easy for researchers to listen to their calls and know which pod is talking.

But because we're such *visually* navigating animals, sonar navigation is for us almost impossible to imagine. It works a lot like sight.

When light bounces off everything, some goes into our eyes, and our brain makes for us an extraordinarily detailed vision of the world around us. We see, in other words, echoes of light.

Imagine being in a dark place with a flashlight, the beam originating from you, bouncing around so you can scan and see what's there. Now imagine that instead of a light beam, your body is producing a beam of sound, and that your brain can still make a detailed assessment of what the beam is bouncing off. Not an image—not visual, perhaps—but enough to tell you with great precision what's there.

Our eyes receive echoes of light, and from that our optic nerves send signals to our brain, and our brain produces images that we see. Eyes and ears only gather light and vibrations. Sights and sounds are created in the brain and experienced in the brain. (With your eyes closed, you can still have mental images of your home, your room, perhaps your favorite pet, and so on. And you can still experience a favorite song. And in dreams your brain also creates images.)

And so it's possible that dolphins' brains might take the impulses from echoes of sound and produce images that the dolphins also experience visually. Yes, it's possible that dolphins such as orcas actually see with sound.

If you imagine the very slow changes over millions of years that turned some mammals into apes and others into whales, we seem to have grown very distant indeed. But is that really a long time, or a big difference? Take the skin off, and the muscles are much the same, the skeletal construction nearly identical. The brain cells, under a microscope, look the same. If you imagine the process very much sped up, you see something real: Dolphins and humans, having shared a long history as animals, vertebrates, and mammals—the same bones and organs doing the same jobs, the same placenta and that same warm milk—are basically the same, in merely shape-shifted proportions. As I've said, it's a little like one person outfitted for hiking and another for scuba diving.

Whales are nearly identical to us in every way except their outer contours. Even their hand bones are identical to ours, just shaped a little differently and hidden in mittens. And dolphins still use those hidden hands for handlike gestures of touch and calming reassurance. And inside our cells? Pretty much the same structures with the same functions, down to amoebas, sequoias, and Portobello mushrooms.

As you peel off layers of difference, you encounter deeper *similarities*. The extreme shrinkage of hind limbs that granted whales their swimming bodies was largely accomplished by the loss of *one* gene. In your body, this *same* gene gave you "normal" limbs. Normal for a human, that is.

If you look at side-by-side drawings of human, elephant, and dolphin brains, the similarities overwhelm the differences. We are essentially the same, merely molded into different outer shapes for coping with different outer surroundings, and wired inside for special talents and abilities. But beneath the skin, as I like to say, we are kin. There is no other animal like us. But don't forget: There are no other animals like each of them, either.

CHAPTER 17

Diverse Minds

I step onto Ken's boat with his assistants Kathy Babiak and Dave Ellifrit. We've barely cleared the harbor when we come startlingly face-to-face with about fifteen or twenty killer whales. This close, their size is alarming. Five times as long as a human, they weigh more than a hundred times what we weigh.

T-20 had just eaten a seal. But the people in the tiny boat know that free-living orcas don't bother humans.

Surging along, their heads push piles and pillows of water, their rising backs so wide that I watch the sea pouring off like water sheeting off an awning. Males, with their huge dorsal and pectoral fins and their immense size, can weigh around 20,000 pounds and be up to 30 feet long; females weigh about two-thirds as much and don't grow quite as long. Traveling, they leave their breaths lingering in the air behind them. Their beauty and momentum are so awe-inspiring that I just silently stare.

There are others ahead. The thirty-five fish-eating residents here right now are the entire L pod. This high-finned adult male with the nick halfway up his dorsal's leading edge and the two nicks on its trailing edge is L-41; he's thirty-six years old. The female pushing just to his left, L-22, is now forty-two years old. Many killer whales have lived past their fifties. One, the matriarch J-2, often called Granny, lived to about one hundred!

Killer whales seem to delight in babies, Dave says. As with elephants and humans, babies make families more active. One thing unusual about killer whales is that females stop giving birth around age forty, but can live another forty years or so past that. We might not see that as unusual because humans are like that, too. But only humans, killer whales, and short-finned pilot whales are known to have this kind of life pattern. (In all other mammals and many other animals, females appear to be capable of breeding right into their old age.)

What do killer whales do with all that granny time? Exactly that:

They become professional grandmothers. They share food with their sons, daughters, and grandchildren. And they lead in decisions about where the family will go and what they'll do. In fact, grandmother orcas remain very important for their family's survival. While they're around, the family does much better, survival-wise.

All members of an orca family are very important for one another. When L-85 was three years old, his mother died. His grown-up brother paid particular attention to him after that. "You'd see this little three-year-old just traveling along beside this massive male," Ken recalls, "almost like a mom." L-85 is now twenty-two years old.

Here comes lucky L-87. He's twenty-one years old. After his mother died eight years ago at age fifty, he survived. "He's got a lot of personality," Ken says. "He's always spy-hopping, sticking his head out to look around at the boats. Sometimes suddenly—*phoosh!*—here he is with his head up right alongside, obviously playing. He likes the reaction of the people. He has a sense of humor. They're not all like that."

"There have been times when a mom would surface on every side of the boat with her newborn, as if showing off to us," Dave adds. Mother killer whales have even temporarily parked babies at the boat while they swam off a short distance to fish or just socialize. Dave was drifting along with J pod once "when the moms with little kids came and said basically, 'Okay—here. Now y'all play around this boat.' So we had four or five kids, one to six years, playing around the boat while their moms went off foraging."

Ken adds, "The kids had a great ol' time romping up to the bow and coming around the stern. They just play with each other like crazy, jumping all over each other."

Right after birth, several females often help bring a newborn to the surface for its first breath. Mothers with little babies frequently push them around on their snouts. One researcher saw three killer whales balancing a newborn in the air on their noses. (Quite a feat, since newborn killer whales measure eight feet long and weigh about four hundred pounds.) Tooth marks on a recent J-pod newborn suggest that a family member may have acted as midwife, helping pull the infant from its mother.

I'm told that adolescent female dolphins, like adolescent elephants and many human teens, are "very, very interested in babysitting or being near babies."

When the whales pass certain land points where people line up clapping and shouting, Ken claims, "the whales get much more excited and acrobatic and really put on a show." People will be running along the shoreline and the whales will flap their tails and slap their fins and jump. Same if they're near whale-watching boats with people cheering."

Why? "Because," he says, "I think we're as entertaining to them as they are to us."

As researcher Diana Reiss has written, "There is someone in there. It's not a human, but it is a someone."

CHAPTER 18

Brain Power

Species who have the most complex societies develop the most complex brains.

If you're going to have a larger, denser brain, you're going to have to pay to run it. And brains are real energy hogs. At just about 2 percent of our body weight, ours uses nearly 20 percent of our body's energy budget (that's why mere thinking can be so tiring). In hard times if you run out of calories, you starve. So why risk having a big brain?

If you have to keep track of specific individuals you meet repeatedly, individuals who might want your food or your mate or your rank and who might plot against you, or might plot with you against your rivals, or be there for you when it matters—you need a social brain capable of reasoning, planning, rewarding, punishing, protecting, bonding, understanding, sympathizing. Your brain needs to be your Swiss Army knife, packing different strategies for different situations. Dolphins, apes, elephants, wolves, and humans face similar needs: Know your territory and its resources, know your friends, monitor your enemies, raise babies, defend, and cooperate when it serves you.

Take-home: The most intelligent brain is *the social brain.*

Twenty-five million years before today, dolphins were firmly in possession of our solar system's brightest brain. In many ways it would be nice if they still were. When dolphins were the planet's brain leaders, the world didn't have any political, religious, ethnic, or environmental problems. Creating problems seems to be one of the things that "makes us human."

And speaking of things believed to "make us human"—. Toolmaking was thought to be exclusively human until researchers found other species who make tools. And *teaching* was also thought to be exclusively human. Yet killer whales teach. "Teaching" means this: One individual takes time from their own task to demonstrate and instruct, *and* the student must learn a new skill.

Around the Indian Ocean's sub-Antarctic Crozet Islands, killer whales capture fur seal and elephant seal pups by surging onto beaches. But it's dangerous. The whales risk stranding themselves and must thrash their bodies back into the rescuing surf. So adults teach the young how to do it. They teach in steps, giving lessons.

First, they practice on beaches without seals. Mothers gently push their young onto steeply sloping beaches, from which youngsters can easily wriggle back into the sea. This teaching builds skills in a safe environment, eliminating the very real risk of a fatal stranding. Then the young learn hunting by watching their mothers' successful attacks. At five to six years old, young killer whales finally attempt to catch seal pups using the beach-surge technique. An adult female often helps them return to the water, creating a body wave if necessary. The time required for teaching means that mothers catch fewer seals for themselves. This training may well be the absolute height in both teaching and long-range planning among non-humans.

In Alaska, researchers saw two killer whales teaching a one-year-old to hunt by practicing on seabirds. Adults stunned an unsuspecting seabird with their flukes; the yearling whale came and practiced the fluke-slapping technique. Atlantic spotted dolphin mothers sometimes release a prey fish and let their youngsters chase the fish. If it's getting away, adults catch it again. Atlantic spotted dolphin youngsters also position themselves alongside mothers who are scanning and prodding sandy bottoms for hidden fish. They can "eavesdrop" on her echoes and imitate her technique, and the mother spends extra time demonstrating. Australian bottlenose dolphin mothers who wear snout sponges to protect against urchin spines and the sting of hidden scorpionfish teach their children the sponge-wearing technique.

Teachers are an elite group. Other teachers include cheetahs and house cats (who bring back live prey and let their young learn to catch it), birds called pied babblers (who teach their young a call that means "I have food"), peregrine falcons (who lure their young away from nesting cliffs before dropping killed prey for them to catch in flight), river otters (who drag their babies into and under water, teaching them how to swim and dive), and meerkats (who first bring to their growing youngsters dead scorpions, then disabled ones, to demonstrate how to dismember the venomous stingers). Humans teach, of course. We know of few other teachers, so far. But many more must be out there.

Like teaching, *imitation*—a sign of high intelligence—is also rare in the animal kingdom.

Yet in South Africa a captive bottlenose dolphin named Daan had watched divers cleaning algae off his pool's windows. He found a gull feather and started cleaning the window, using the same long strokes. He positioned himself vertically, with one flipper touching the glass— like the divers, who'd steadied themselves by holding on to the window frame—and made sounds almost identical to the diver's breathing apparatus, and released a similar-looking stream of bubbles.

In a South African aquarium lived a baby Indo-Pacific bottlenose named Dolly. One day when she was just six months old, Dolly was watching a trainer standing at the window smoking a cigarette, blowing puffs of smoke. Dolly swam to her mother, briefly suckled, then returned to the window and released a cloud of milk that engulfed her head. The trainer was "absolutely astonished." Somehow Dolly *came up with the idea* of using milk to *represent* smoke. Using one thing to represent something else isn't just mimicking. It is art.

CHAPTER 19

Defying Explanation

"I've sometimes come away," Ken says, "with a real *'Wow!'* feeling. Like I'd just seen something above and beyond. When you lock eyes with them, you get the sense that they're looking at *you*. It's a steady gaze. And you feel it. Much more powerful than a dog looking at you. A lot transmits in a very brief time about the intent of both sides."

Like what?

"In those looks I've felt"—he hesitates—"appreciated. But of course," he quickly adds, "that's subjective."

Appreciated?

Ken started his research in the 1970s, right after the courts ordered SeaWorld to stop catching baby whales. "Within a year or so," Ken says, "if someone in another boat started chasing the whales each time they surfaced, they would often come over and just stay around our boat. They saw," he says, "that we were cool around them. Which implies, y'know, a consciousness of what's going on."

Ken has stories like this one: "For days we'd been following all three pods. One morning, they were headed into a dense fog bank. We followed them. This was in the 1970s. No GPS or anything, just a compass. We got lost down near the entrance to Admiralty Inlet, socked-in fog, about twenty-five miles from home. I knew the approximate compass bearing. We put away all the cameras and prepared to run. I started to head along that compass bearing at about fifteen knots. We'd only gone for about five minutes when whales just came in from all directions until they were right in front of the boat. So I just slowed down and followed wherever they went. I had about half a dozen of them right in front of our bow at all times." Ken followed them for fifteen miles. When the fog opened, he could see his home island.

"Well," he says, "I do have the feeling that they knew absolutely that we had zero visibility. They knew exactly where they were. It was the year after the captures ended. They'd seen lots of boats and been subject to a lot of aggressive behavior. But there they were, and as far as I can tell, they were guiding us. It was very touching."

It gets, if anything, more touching. And much stranger. Killer whales seem capable of random acts of kindness. Acts that defy explanation. Acts that make scientists consider some pretty far-out possibilities. One might conclude that killer whale behavior falls into two categories: amazing behavior and unexplained behavior.

Once, Alexandra Morton and an assistant were out in the open water of Queen Charlotte Strait in her inflatable boat when she was enveloped by fog so thick she felt like she was "in a glass of milk." No compass. No view of the sun. A wrong hunch about the direction home would have brought them out into open ocean. Worse, a giant cruise ship was moving closer in fog so reflective Alexandra could not tell where its sound was approaching from. She imagined it suddenly splitting the fog before it crushed them.

Then, as if from nowhere, a smooth black fin popped up. Top Notch. Then Saddle. And then Eve, the usually aloof matriarch. Sharky was suddenly peeking at her. Then Stripe. As they clumped close around her tiny boat, Alexandra followed them in the fog like a blind person with a hand on their shoulder. "I never worried," she recalled. "I trusted them with our lives." Twenty minutes later, she saw a materializing outline of their island's massive cedars and rocky shoreline. The fog opened up. The whales left them. Earlier in the day, the whales had been unusually difficult to follow and had been traveling west, toward open ocean. The whales had taken Alexandra south, to her home. When the whales left, they changed direction, aiming back toward where they'd just come from and where they had originally been headed.

Alexandra felt changed. "For more than twenty years, I have fought to keep the mythology of the orcas out of my work. When others would regale a group with stories of an orca's sense of humor or music appreciation, I'd hold my tongue.... Yet there are times when I am confronted with profound evidence of something beyond our ability to scientifically quantify. Call them amazing coincidences if you like; for me they keep adding up.... I have no explanation for that day's events.

I have only gratitude and a deep sense of mystery that continues to grow."

There are stories of killer whales seemingly retrieving lost dogs. A small party of researchers left shore to go whale watching in a small boat. When they returned, their German shepherd, Phoenix, was not on the island. He'd apparently tried to follow them out into the big water and powerful tides of Johnstone Strait. The people searched the strait until eleven p.m. No dog. The dog's owner was sitting on a log, crying, when he heard the blows of killer whales coming. Just after the whales passed, he heard splashing. Suddenly, there stood his sodden dog, weak and vomiting salt water. "I don't care what people say," he declared. "Those whales saved my dog."

It's not an isolated case. At a different research camp, a person went kayaking, and when he returned, *his* dog, named Karma, was missing. Similarly, she'd probably tried to follow him. The researcher was mourning the loss of his faithful companion late in the night when some whales passed. The dog appeared on the beach, soaked and trembling and near collapse. "I was there," said the person who related the story. "There's no doubt in my mind; those whales had pushed Karma ashore."

Decades earlier, while watching two captive whales named Orky and Corky swim around their pool at Marineland of the Pacific one day, Alexandra had asked a trainer to show her how one teaches a new idea to a whale. (Corky was the captured child of Stripe. Many years later, in the incident I mentioned a few paragraphs ago, Stripe would help lead Alexandra home in the fog.) Neither Alexandra nor the trainer had ever seen either captive whale slap their dorsal fin on the water. They decided they'd work on that trick the following week. "Then something happened," Alexandra later wrote, "that has made me careful of my thoughts around whales ever since." *Corky slapped her dorsal fin on the water's surface.* She did it several more times, then charged around the tank, exuberantly smacking the water with her dorsal fin. "That's whales for you," said the trainer, smiling. "They can read your mind. We trainers see this kind of stuff all the time."

Luna was a little male born to L pod's Splash in 1999. Then, in the spring of 2001, Luna went missing.

He showed up alone, barely more than a toddler of two years old, in British Columbia's Nootka Sound. But he was far inside a long bay, where he wouldn't be able to hear his pod's calls.

Orcas teach, and they share most of their catches

He was lost, and he was also at a loss for company. He'd catch a salmon and then hold it in the air. "He was certainly showing us what he had caught," one person opined. "You realize," said another, "this is not a reptile.... This is somebody."

One recreational fisherman said that when he first encountered Luna, he put his hand underwater and waved it, "so he puts his fin above the water and he is waving back at me." Convinced that this must be a coincidence, the fisherman waved again. Luna waved again. Luna left for a few minutes, and when he returned, the fisherman waved once more. Sure enough, Luna waved back. "Here is something," the fisherman realized, "that has got way more intelligence than the domestic animals that we are used to." When a workboat cook encountered Luna and looked into his eyes, she saw something so astonishing and deep that, she said, "I could not breathe."

As he grew, Luna sought to play with boaters and people of all kinds. He had no problem pushing forty-foot logs or turning a thirty-foot sailboat in a circle. But when he went to play with a canoe paddled by two women, or a kayak, he'd nudge very gently. Could Luna have had any idea that the water, his home medium, would kill a person? Like many things about killer whales and everything about Luna, that seems so unlikely. But what else explains it?

"Luna quickly found," as Ken puts it, "that humans could be a source of pretty interesting interaction." He liked being touched, having humans rub his tongue, getting sprayed with hoses—"all sorts of things you wouldn't think possible with a wild animal," Ken recalls.

Luna showed that he was a social being foremost and deepest, and that being a killer whale was, in a sense, secondary. One Luna observer said that he could "look through your otherness at you."

Luna would hang with a docked boat for hours as the people on it were busy delivering supplies and equipment. But as soon as the people left, he'd leave. Yet if a person remained aboard sleeping, Luna would often stay with the boat all night. One captain frequently heard the sound of Luna's breathing outside his open window. When a passenger's hat blew into the water, Luna went to get it. He came up under it and, with the hat perched perfectly on his head, brought it back within reach. The man got his hat back, thanks to an untrained freeliving whale who showed in so many ways that he, at least, was a good friend.

Michelle Kehler, who'd been hired with a woman named Erin Hobbs as government Luna monitors, recalled, "When he would come up to the boat, there was a lot of eye contact. It was very soft; it was very genuine." She observed, too, that "his relationship with me was different from his relationship with Erin." Erin is the jokester, and Luna joked with her. "He would spit at her. She would get water in the face. She would get all the gross stuff. She would get all the tail slaps, the pec slaps....He never did that with me. And we are on the same boat, like five feet apart....He was totally different with me....We have different energies. He played to that, for sure. And it was amazing."

One day when Luna was playing a little too energetically with the emergency outboard engine on Michael Parfit's boat, Michael asked,

"Hey, Luna, could you leave that alone for a while?" Luna immediately left it alone, and backed away.

Michael wrote, "It was hard to accept that level of awareness and intention in something that did not look in any way human." He added, "A sense washed over me that this orca was just as aware of living as I was: that he could perceive all the details that I perceive, the feeling of atmosphere and sea, the texture of emotions . . . and what makes us feel safe. This was overwhelming."

Eventually, Michael realized that he had finally looked through the otherness. He no longer saw something that didn't look human. He didn't see a killer whale. He saw Luna.

When the trainer at Marineland of the Pacific said that killer whales can read your mind, she wasn't joking. But what if she wasn't just serious—what if she was right? What if, like their sonar abilities, which weren't suspected until the 1950s, there's another unknown-to-us modality to their communication and perception? I seriously doubt it. But here's a thought: Science fiction used to imagine wise visitors from outer space wielding huge heads housing vastly superior brainpower. The whales certainly have, at least, very big heads.

In the 1960s, Karen Pryor discovered that rough-toothed dolphins could understand the concept "Do something new." If she rewarded them when they did something they'd never been taught or had never done, at a specific signal they "thought of things to do spontaneously that we could never have imagined."

When the Hawaiian bottlenose dolphins Phoenix and Akeakamai got the signal to "do something new," they would swim to the center of the pool and circle underwater for a few seconds, then do something entirely unexpected. For instance, they might both shoot straight up through the surface in perfect unison and spin clockwise while squirting water from their mouths. None of that performance was trained.

"It looks to us absolutely mysterious," researcher Louis Herman related. "We don't know how they do it." It *seems* as if they communicate using some form of language to plan and execute a complex new stunt. If there's another way of doing it, or what that might be, or whether there's some other way to communicate that humans can't quite imagine—dolphin telepathy?—no human knows. Whatever it is, for the dolphins it's apparently as routine and natural as human kids saying, "Hey, let's do this..."

In Argentina, when park ranger Roberto Bubas stepped into the water and played his harmonica, the same individual killer whales who catch and eat sea lions along the shore would form a ring around him like puppies. They'd rally playfully around his kayak and come as he called to them.

Free-living killer whales treat humans with a strange lack of violence. It's especially strange when compared with the rate at which humans continue hurting and killing other humans. How to explain *either* fact? For the sea's *T. rex* to stick its head up alongside a tiny boat many times and *never* hurt a human even in play—that begs for an explanation. More crucially, it demands that we find a way to understand. Perhaps one day.

Many stories show other whales being gentle. Photographer Bryant Austin had been photographing humpback whale mothers and babies when a five-week-old infant left his mother and swam up to him, less than a foot away. Bryant suddenly felt a firm tap on his shoulder. "As I turned to look, I was suddenly eye to eye with the calf's mother. She had extended the tip of her two-ton, fifteen-foot-long pectoral fin and positioned it in such a way as to gently touch my shoulder." Realizing that he was now between the mother and her baby, he was frightened by the thought that she could easily break his back. Instead, Bryant described her actions as "delicate."

Meanwhile, the baby swam over to biologist Libby Eyre. The young whale rolled underneath Libby and then gently lifted her out of the water on his belly. She was on her hands and knees looking down at his throat. The young whale placed his pectoral fin on her back, then gently rolled and put her back in the sea.

CHAPTER 20

Helping in Mind

Free-living killer whales don't hurt humans.
But they do hunt seals. And sometimes when they do, humpback
whales help the seals. After killer whales washed a Weddell seal off an
ice floe, whale experts Bob Pitman and John Durban watched as the
seal dashed toward two nearby humpback whales. "Just as the seal got
to the closest humpback, the huge animal rolled over on its back—and
the four-hundred-pound seal was swept up onto the humpback's chest
between its massive flippers. Then, as the killer whales moved in closer,
the humpback arched its chest, lifting the seal out of the water." When
the seal started sliding back into the sea, "the humpback gave the seal
a gentle nudge with its flipper, back to the middle of its chest." Shortly
thereafter, the seal scrambled off, swimming to safety on a nearby
ice floe.

Sometimes whales and dolphins seem to know they need help
from humans, and they seem to appreciate it. A humpback whale off
San Francisco got tangled in dozens of crab traps connected by about

Some Antarctic killer whales eat seals (Photo by Robert Pitman)

a mile of rope, with weights every sixty feet; all the gear weighed over a thousand pounds. Rope was wrapped at least four times around the whale's tail, back, mouth, and left front flipper, cutting into the giant's flesh. Though nearly fifty feet long and weighing about fifty tons, the whale was being pulled down and was having trouble breathing when divers got into the water to see whether they could help. The first diver was so aghast at the extent of the entanglement, he didn't think they'd be able to free the whale. Further, he feared that the whale's thrashing could entangle the divers, too. But instead of struggling to break away as soon as possible, the whale remained passive through an entire hour while the divers worked. "When I was cutting the line going through the mouth," James Moskito said, "its eye was there winking at me, watching me. It was an epic moment of my life." When the whale realized it was free, it did not swim away. Instead, it swam to the closest diver, nuzzled him, then swam to the next one. "It stopped about a foot away from me, pushed me around a little bit and had some fun," James told a *San Francisco Chronicle* reporter. "It felt to me like it was thanking us, knowing that it was free and that we had helped it. It seemed kind of affectionate, like a dog that's happy to see you."

A video on YouTube shows a dolphin off Hawaii with a fishhook in its flipper, actively seeking aid from scuba divers. How does a dolphin with a fishhook in its flipper decide to seek help from a human diver, a creature so alien in the history of its realm? Would it seek help from a turtle or a fish? Doubtful. Another dolphin? It seemed to understand its problem as well as we might. But can dolphins really understand that we, like them, understand—*and* that we have these *hands that can remove a hook?* Apparently, yes.

Dolphins and other animals who seek our help possess a mind that understands that humans, too, have a mind and can help (if we choose to). To understand that we might understand is more than we often grant to them.

In Baja, Mexico, I experienced mother gray whales swimming up to the boat with newborns, as if proudly presenting them to us, and standing by while we stroked them. Our guides, Don Pachico Mayoral and his son Jesus, explained that if they come and you don't stroke them, they leave. Whatever their motivation or reason, they are seeking contact with humans.

There are many stories recounting dolphins pushing distressed swimmers to the surface. My editor Jack Macrae was kayaking off the Georgia coast when the wind and tide changed and conditions became challenging. He was beginning to grow worried. Soon dolphins appeared, flanking him. He went with them, and they brought him to an inlet where he could get to safety. When a researcher swimming in the waters of the Bahamas got tired and needed to be towed by another crew member, an Atlantic spotted dolphin suddenly stopped what she was doing and immediately escorted them to their boat. On a sailboat off Venezuela in 1997, the crew could not find a sailor who had fallen overboard. About an hour later, searchers in a powerboat saw two dolphins approach and quickly turn away, approach and quickly turn away, several times. The captain had already searched in that direction. But he decided to follow. They found the sailor, alive—attended by dolphins. One foggy day, biologist Maddalena Bearzi was taking notes on a familiar party of nine bottlenose dolphins who'd cleverly encircled a school of sardines near the Malibu pier. "Just after they began feeding," she writes, "one of the dolphins in the group suddenly left the circle, swimming offshore at a high speed. In less than an instant, the other dolphins left their prey to follow." To abruptly stop feeding— that was pretty odd. Maddalena followed, too. "We were at least three miles offshore when the dolphins stopped suddenly, forming a large ring without exhibiting any specific behavior." That's when Maddalena and her assistants spotted an inert human body with long, blond hair floating in the center of the dolphin ring. "Her face was pale and her lips were blue as I pulled her fully dressed and motionless body from the water." Warmed with blankets and the researchers' bodies, she began to respond. She survived.

CHAPTER 21

The Cost of Captivity

On a late July day in 1965, a killer whale that had been accidentally caught in a fishing net arrived at the Seattle Aquarium. For over a year, Namu, as he was known, proved wildly attractive to ticket buyers. Then he died. He was the first of many.

The aquarium and several other marine-themed parks wanted more. The first live-capture operation was mounted jointly by SeaWorld and the Seattle Aquarium in October 1965. Catchers were free to take as many young whales as they wanted. No one understood anything about their social structures. What was the harm in snagging a few for the tanks?

Between the early 1960s and the mid-1970s, many individual killer whales got netted repeatedly by catchers intent on taking their young ones from them. A quarter of the live-captured whales had bullet wounds from random shootings. This was the relationship between humans and the Northwest's whales. The Northwest's whales began avoiding some of their favorite, most food-rich places, which had turned so dangerous. Then public sentiment began souring on the captures.

Ultimately, researchers documented—beyond doubt—that fewer than 150 southern resident whales swam these waters. Their work probably prevented the group's extinction. Counting whales taken alive and others killed during netting activities, the captures removed about 40 percent of the population—roughly 60 whales. In 1975 and 1976, Canada and Washington State, at least, finally banned killer whale captures.

The whales had not changed. It's just that in watching whales performing and interacting with trainers, we, for the first time, got a world-altering glimpse of them. In those days, whale watching didn't exist. Wildlife films were just getting started.

The performing whales had been taken from their families, and from their freedom. From them, we learned that "killer whales" are not mindless killers but rather are sensitive, interactive, careful gentle giants. So the question is: Was the sacrifice of those performing whales worth the changed public understanding?

To answer that, we have to see what it cost the whales.

As killer whales became moneymakers, aquariums and amusement parks wanted more and more. The captivity business shifted into high gear.

In the gripping film *Blackfish*, Howard Garrett, an advocate for the whales, recalls one particular chase during the 1970s. Speedboats were hurling explosives to frighten a group of whales toward the net boats. But these orcas had been caught before, he explains, "and they knew what was going on, and they knew their young ones would be taken from them. So the adults without young went east, into a cul-de-sac. And the boats followed them, thinking they were all going that way."

But the adults with babies had split off, shepherding their young ones around the far side of an island. The ones without young made themselves obvious; the ones with the babies stealthily slipped away. It seemed a tactically brilliant strategy, confronting us with a question we've faced before: *How* might they have communicated such thinking?

But as Howard reminds us, "they have to come up for air eventually." And when they did, the catchers' aircraft spotted them. So the speedboats caught them there. After they had the young ones penned, the catchers slacked the main net so the older ones could swim off.

They didn't leave.

"As the catchers began lassoing the babies," Ken tells me, "mothers would vigorously try to prevent their babies from being taken. The mom would get in between and try to push the baby away. There'd be a lot of squealing." As Ken recalls it, catchers afraid for their safety sometimes simply killed resisting adults.

Diver John Crowe picks up the narrative in the film. While they were maneuvering a baby into a stretcher for removal, he recalls, "the whole fam-damily is twenty-five yards away in a big line, communicating back and forth. Well, you understand then what you're doing. I lost it. I just started crying.…Just like kidnapping a little kid away from its mother.…I can't think of anything worse than that." He finished the job, though: "Everybody's watching; what can you do?" When it was all over, the net held three dead whales. John and two others were directed to "cut the whales open, fill 'em with rocks, put anchors on their tails, and sink 'em." John says that what he did that day was "the worst thing I've ever done."

It's impossible to imagine the mental experience of a social mammal with a brain comparable to ours who has just tried her best to prevent her child from being taken, has failed, and is swimming away from the chaos bereft of her small one, with whom, for the last few years, she has been in constant touch. For the baby, isolated, suddenly cut off from her family's voices, going from the limitless ocean to the confinement of a concrete teacup, the terror and confusion.

SeaWorld eventually succeeded in getting babies out of its captive whales. But they didn't keep the mothers and their surviving children together, as is normal for orcas. Instead, SeaWorld's management removed the young ones soon after weaning and shipped them among their chain of theme parks as if they were stuffed toys.

Former SeaWorld trainer Carol Ray tells her interviewer in *Blackfish* that after the SeaWorld staff took Katina's baby, Katina "stayed in the corner of the pool, literally shaking and screaming, screeching, crying. I'd never seen her do anything like that.…There is nothing that you could call that besides grief." Former SeaWorld trainer John Hargrove remembers Kasatka and her baby as "very close...inseparable." After the baby had been taken to the airport, Kasatka "continued to make vocalizations that had never been heard before." A research scientist who analyzed the sounds concluded that Kasatka was making long-range calls, trying to establish contact with her missing child.

Howard Garrett reminds us in the film that when killer whales were first brought into captivity, we knew less than nothing; they were considered vicious killers. But we've learned that "they're amazingly friendly and understanding and intuitively want to be your companion."

Imagine captivity in reverse. Imagine yourself captured around age four, raised by whales who find you fascinating. Your language learning would end. Normal socialization would end. The known world would shrink to a single room surrounded by whales looking in at you. Your memories of the wider world and your family would fade. You would get your meals by putting your head underwater to take handouts from fascinated keepers. None of those keepers would have ever seen humans living normally in human families. They'd learn a little something from almost everything you did. Your own education, in any meaningful sense, would have been terminated. You would no longer be part of the world. You'd be only an amusing little part of their world. As a youngster, you'd find them interesting. Anyway, interacting with them would be almost all the stimulation you'd ever get. You'd certainly need stimulation. The whales would fill some of your loneliness. You would not exactly understand what you were missing, but your basic needs for human fulfillment would be going unmet. The routine would get boring. Inevitably, you wouldn't be quite right. Imagine a life spent in a circular room with blank walls. Round and round you go.

Orcas are born and built for a complex world of long-distance sound and long-distance travel. They remain with their mothers and siblings their entire lives. They maintain long-distance relationships, too, with occasional reunions with dozens of other individuals whom they know for their whole long lives. Then we put them in concrete pools that function as both isolation quarters and echo chambers. What does that do to a whale's growing mind?

The theme parks and aquariums that describe their captives as "ambassadors" have a point. What they could use, though, is a heart.

In 1978, in captivity, Corky gave birth. She'd given birth a few years earlier; her first baby had lived a few weeks, then died. The small tank required tight circling, but the baby couldn't make the maneuver, so Corky kept preventing her baby from bumping into the wall. This continually put Corky's face next to her baby; the baby was never in the position of following alongside that would properly present the mother's teats for nursing. After a week of difficult force-feeding by handlers, the baby was looking thin. Management thought they might feed the baby better if it was in a shallower pool. Handlers put the baby in a sling, and a crane pulled the sling into the air. Alexandra Morton was there: "As her baby's voice left the water and entered the air, the mother threw her enormous body against the tank walls, again and again, causing the entire stadium to shake. I burst into tears. Corky slammed her body for about an hour."

Alexandra, an expert on whale sound, recalled that the night Corky's baby was taken, the mother kept repeating a new and different sound. This sound was "strident, guttural, and urgent." After each breath, Corky returned to the bottom of the tank. There she resumed her lament. The baby's father, Orky, circled, occasionally uttering staccato, gunshot-like echolocation sounds. Alexandra listened to this for three days, as "Corky's calls grew hoarse."

At dawn on the fourth day, Corky grew silent, rose, took a breath, and called, *Pituuuuuuu*. Her mate returned the same call, and the whales began moving and breathing in unison. When the trainers arrived, Corky ate for the first time since her baby was removed.

Grief, mourning, recovering—but not forgetting. After that, Corky began lying by a window with a view of gift-shop merchandise. For hours she'd stay there—next to a stack of toy stuffed orcas. Did the toys remind her of her lost children? Did she think that somewhere in there was her lost baby?

Corky got pregnant again. Then one day, she, whose exquisite sonar allowed her to avoid any obstacle, shattered a three-quarters-of-an-inch-thick glass window of her tank. The window that she burst was the one adjacent to the stacks of stuffed-toy killer whales. Was she trying to take her unborn baby out of the tank from which her first babies disappeared? Toward the place where baby orcas rested undisturbed?

The most certain thing we can say is: She knew the tank; she didn't shatter the glass by accident. A few weeks later, her stillborn baby arrived, seven months premature.

Years after Corky shattered the window, a film crew let Corky hear a recording of whales from her remaining free-living pod, her family members. "While her Icelandic pen mates ignored the sounds," wrote Alexandra Morton, "Corky's whole body began shuddering terribly. If she wasn't 'crying,' she was doing something terribly similar."

I'm not saying we've learned nothing from whale captures. Quite the opposite. By holding them close, by challenging the normalcy of their lives and watching them cope, we began seeing them for the first time. And they astounded us. Like learning about the depth and reach of the human spirit by watching human prisoners doing magnificent things to help one another stay alive, we confronted the relational capacities of whales. We learned the most basic thing about them: that they are somebody.

CHAPTER 22

The Big Picture

"The captures in the 1960s and '70s—especially of young whales—*really* mattered," Ken is saying emphatically. "It caused a long-term problem." The young ones were needed to grow into adults and keep the population going. But now, various resident families have *no* living females of reproductive age. For instance, one family is all males except for its matriarch, and she's past menopause. That whole family is doomed.

The southern resident community totaled about 120 whales before the captures; after the captures, it was down to around 70. It started rebuilding, managing to hit 99 whales in the 1990s. But then the rebuild hit a pause. Forty years later, the population—around 80 whales—is declining. They're losing one or two a year.

Canada's northern residents, numbering about 260, were increasing during the last decade. Recently their growth has slowed, perhaps stopped.

"No reproduction—almost none—is what's the bummer," Ken laments. Over 40 percent of babies are dying before they're a year old.

It seems they don't get enough to eat.

First we took their children, then we destroyed their food supply. For the Northwest's fish-eating whales, life's been getting increasingly difficult. Salmon abundance is way, way down.

All ages and both sexes of the whales are perishing at relatively high rates. Present trends will erase these pods in a few decades.

King (chinook) salmon declines appear to be pretty tightly linked with whales dying off. That's not surprising; the residents' diet is 65 percent chinook salmon.

In the good old days, "there were really incredible numbers of fish around," Ken vividly recalls. "You'd have maybe a million and a half sockeye and pink salmon, and several hundred thousand kings swimming by. A lot of kings weighed twenty pounds or more, and the whales would only need about ten fish a day. They'd all hang out together and, I mean, *party down!* They'd push a salmon around with their nose or maybe drape one over their back. All that playful, social stuff would happen right in front of my window."

Not helping: toxic chemicals. Being at the top of the food chain, whales get all the toxic chemicals that concentrate as they move up in the food pyramid from plankton to small fish to big fish to whale. In the first half of the 1900s when the oldest living whales here were born, those toxic chemicals did not exist in the world. In the 1970s, chemicals like DDT and PCBs caused birth defects in Puget Sound seals. Those chemicals were banned, and they're slowly disappearing; that's good. But new chemicals like flame retardants that can weaken immune systems and can disrupt reproductive systems are rising in concentration in the environment.

Ken is a cheerful man. He loves the whales. But he worries that the whales he's devoted his life to might be doomed. And though food shortages and toxic chemicals would be bad enough, there's more.

While I'm at Ken's, I read an e-mail: "The U.S. Navy says it will ignore a unanimous recommendation by the California Coastal Commission to reduce the harmful effects of naval sonar on the state's marine mammals. The Navy is planning to dramatically increase its use of dangerous sonar and high-powered explosives off the coast of Southern California during training and testing. It predicts that such operations will kill hundreds of marine mammals—and injure thousands of others—over the next five years. New research shows that…" The Natural Resources Defense Council is working to stop this, or to get the plan modified.

Ken explains that very high-power, extremely loud military sonar, along with bombing practice in the ocean, has repeatedly killed whales.

They are such wonderful creatures. Just trying to live their lives, as we all are. But we make it so hard for them.

Will we ever really see all these animals, these beings, the elephants and the orcas and the others, for who they are? Will we simply let them exist? These are the big questions.

Today our goal is simpler. It is to try to practice really seeing them for who they are. Our immediate objective is to find and ID some whales we've been hearing about via the radio chatter. In Ken's boat, our propeller drills us into Haro Strait under heavy, fast-moving weather that keeps switching between the rain of autumn and the sunshine of a lingering summer.

Soon, only about a mile from shore and directly off Ken's house, members of both L pod and K pod appear. This is good. So Ken is good. He smiles mischievously and says, "If I didn't have to live ashore, I'd live with them. Go with the flow." He laughs. He's not entirely joking.

As many as fifty whales are moving along at an even clip, southbound, breathing evenly, surfacing with a slight blow, slipping back down, then easing back up.

But despite their apparent effortlessness, the most striking thing about them is their momentum. It seems nearly impossible that these ancient beings, who need so much of what we've taken from them, remain. I can hardly believe that we have overlapped in time and place. I so avidly hope they can last.

Several whales arch their backs and dive steeply. Below, some fish have their attention. A couple of other whales slice rapidly through the surface, quickly switching directions, a maneuver Ken calls "sharking." They're in determined pursuit of salmon. The closest whale, right behind us, is L-92. This big one over here with the high, wavy dorsal fin is K-25. He begins a series of high-arcing lunges, with lots of splashing and commotion. He's after one large, isolated fish. He dives away. When he suddenly bursts through the surface, his mass and momentum startle me wide-eyed.

"See them working toward the shore there?" Ken lays out the scene for me. They're corralling salmon toward the shoreline, concentrating them a bit. "The whales will slowly work the salmon, trying not to panic them, pushing them into bunches while looking for one that might be lagging, or individuals that stray from the group. That's how they do it. Every once in a while, a fish will get a little behind or too far from its school. They'll nail it." We make the rounds so Ken can complete today's cataloging. It's so extraordinary to be doing our task among these whales who are so actively working and feeding.

Here we have, he tells me, K-22, K-25, K-37, L-83, L-116.... He knows *who* they are. He knows *where* they have been. He knows their lives because their lives have been his life. They *are* his life at this very moment. As for being among lunging, hungry, hunting killer whales— there is nothing at all for us to fear. So I don't.

As for Ken, he's concentrating deeply as he wields his camera.

Then the sky begins flecking us with raindrops that crowd to a steady drizzle, sizzling the surrounding water. Ken acknowledges the rain and says, "Okay, we're done. I've ruined enough cameras. Tomorrow's another day."

But, cameras stowed, we linger. In the rain, we watch. For a while, everywhere in the near and medium distance, black fins continue urgently scribbling their stories on the slate of the sea. I read them as intently as I can, knowing that the sea will soon erase what they have written, and that we don't have a backup file.

Orca whales. They might all look the same in a photo, but scientists know each individual by name. And the orcas themselves know each other individually.

EPILOGUE

Anyone who studies a wild animal faces the challenge of, in effect, making a case for its life on earth. I pray that mine is strong enough.

—Alexandra Morton

Just as all humans are the same and each human differs, all species are the same and each species differs from all others. And within that, each creature, too, is an individual. It is a matter of mystery and delight that so many species can bridge that boundary between us, so that the hawk looks for the falconer, the dog seeks its human companion, the elephant stands vigil over the injured man, and the killer whale playfully shoves a sailboat but gives a kayak the gentlest nudge.

We are all so similar under the skin. Four limbs, the same bones, the same organs, the same origins, and lots of shared history. And we do what it takes, to the best of our abilities, to stay alive and keep the babies alive, to live out the mystery of life and existence.

Almost all people who study the behavior of other animals justify their interest by saying that it helps us understand ourselves. It does. But much more important, it helps us understand other animals. We need to know them. And they very much need for us to know them.

What I've tried to show is how other animals experience the lives they so energetically hold on to. I wanted to know *who* these creatures are. Now we may feel, beneath our ribs, why they must live.

Ours is the species that best understands the world, yet has the worst relationship with it. Usually we see the whole universe through a human lens. The most beautiful human moments might be when, once in a while, we see ourselves *not* in a mirror but from a distance. It's when our minds consider us from outside ourselves, looking back at where and how we live, helping us understand who we are, and our place in things.

The greatest thing our human minds are capable of understanding is: All life is one.

NOTES

Part One: Lives of Elephants

Chapter 2: Seeing Elephants

6 *area roughly twenty times larger:* Moss et al., *Amboseli Elephants,* p. 89.

9 *"Imagine having a nose":* Yoshihito Niimura quoted in Feltman, R. 2014. "New Study Finds That Elephants Evolved the Most Discerning Nose of Any Mammal." *Washington Post,* July 22.

Chapter 3: The Same Basic Brain

15 *"understanding third-party relationships":* Oliveira et al. 1998, as cited in Moss et al., *Amboseli Elephants,* p. 179.

16 *the thing that feels like something:* Koch, C. 2014. "Ubiquitous Minds." *Scientific American Mind* 25(1): 26–29.

19 *"deep and very ancient circuits":* Panksepp, J. 2005. "Affective Consciousness: Core Emotional Feelings in Animals and Humans." *Consciousness and Cognition* 14(1): 30–80.

Chapter 4: We Are Family

21 *Elephant brains:* Moss, *Elephant Memories,* p. 265.

21 *The family is the foundation:* Moss et al., *Amboseli Elephants,* p. 190.

22 *Lucy Bates collected some urine:* Ibid., p. 176.

26 *Each elephant in Amboseli probably knows:* Ibid., p. 211.

27 *Eventually their teeth wear down:* Moss, *Elephant Memories,* p. 245.

27 *devastating psychological consequences* and *extraordinarily close care bonds:* Ibid., p. 322.

28 *Older orphans sometimes wander:* Moss et al., *Amboseli Elephants,* p. 320.

Chapter 5: Motherhood Happens

33 *they suck their trunk for comfort:* Moss, *Elephant Memories,* pp. 161–62.

33 *babies reach into the mouths:* Ibid., pp. 164–65.

Chapter 6: Playing for Fun

38 *loose and "floppy" way:* Moss, *Elephant Memories,* p. 122.

Chapter 7: Elephant Empathy

40 *Cherie pursued her:* Douglas-Hamilton, I., S. Bhalla, G. Wittemyer, and F. Vollrath. 2006. "Behavioural Reactions of Elephants Towards a Dying and Deceased Matriarch." *Applied Animal Behaviour Science* 100(1–2): 87–102.

40 *baby who could not straighten:* Moss and Colbeck, *Echo of the Elephants,* pp. 64–74.

41 *"carefully and ever so slowly":* Ibid., p. 72.

42 *Suddenly he panicked:* Ibid., p. 37.

42 *"Elephants show empathy":* Moss et al., *Amboseli Elephants,* p. 182.

43 *half-blind Turkana woman:* Douglas-Hamilton and Douglas-Hamilton, *Among the Elephants,* p. 240.

Chapter 8: Good Grief

45 *recording of an elephant who had died:* Vicki Fishlock, resident scientist at the Amboseli Elephant Research Project (AERP), personal communication, July 2013.

45 *"probably the strangest thing about them":* Moss, *Elephant Memories,* p. 270.

45 *"it is their silence that is most unsettling"*: Poole, *Coming of Age with Elephants,* p. 159.

46 *the parts that would have been most familiar:* Moss, *Elephant Memories,* p. 270. See also Moss and Colbeck, *Echo of the Elephants,* p. 61.

46 *"a strange habit of removing"*: Sheldrick quoted in Douglas-Hamilton and Douglas-Hamilton, *Among the Elephants,* p. 237.

47 *plastered his large head wound:* Ibid., pp. 240–41.

48 *In a zoo in Philadelphia:* Brown, A. E. 1879. "Grief in the Chimpanzee." *American Naturalist,* March, 173–75.

48 *More than a century later:* de Waal, F. 2013. "Bonobo Bliss: Evidence That Doing Good Feels Good." *Natural History,* August 8. Excerpted from de Waal, *Bonobo and Atheist.*

48 *Two male chimpanzees in Uganda:* Zimmer, C. 2012. "Friends with Benefits." *Time.* February 20.

48 *Patricia Wright studies:* Dr. Patricia Wright, American primatologist, anthropologist, and conservationist, personal conversation, September 2014. See also Radin, D. 2014. "The Amazing Emotional Intelligence of Our Primate Cousins." *Ecologist,* June 24.

49 *The two brothers spent days:* Simmonds, M. P. 2006. "Into the Brains of Whales." *Applied Animal Behaviour Science* 100(1–2): 103–16.

Chapter 9: Elephant Talk

51 *"If someone in the family"*: Moss et al., *Amboseli Elephants,* pp. 116, 155.

52 *During high social excitement:* Ibid., p. 115.

53 *Elephant song spans ten octaves:* Ibid., p. 130.

53 *Rumbles during tense encounters:* Ibid., p. 127.

54 *Meaning often depends on context:* Moss et al., *Amboseli Elephants,* p. 158.

54 *Elephants use well over one hundred:* Ibid., p. 109. See also ElephantVoices.org

55 *their word for "Bees!":* King, L. E., I. Douglas-Hamilton, and F. Vollrath. 2007. "African Elephants Run from the Sound of Disturbed Bees." *Current Biology* 17(19): R832–33. See also Bouché, P., et al. 2011. "Will Elephants Soon Disappear from West African Savannahs?" *PLoS ONE* 6(6): e20619.

55 *Aauurrrr* and *Some rumbles by mothers:* Ibid., pp. 147, 148, 149, 158.

56 *"Hello, it's good to be near you again":* Ibid., p. 151.

Chapter 10: It's Going to Be Tough

57 *In camp this morning:* Wittemyer, G., et al. 2014. "Illegal Killing for Ivory Drives Global Decline in African Elephants." *Current Biology* 111: 13117–21. See also Scriber, B. 2014. "100,000 Elephants Killed by Poachers in Just Three Years, Landmark Analysis Finds." *National Geographic News,* August 14.

Chapter 11: Ivory

67 *From an estimated ten million elephants:* Bradshaw, G. A., et al. 2005. "Elephant Breakdown." *Nature* 433: 807.

68 *30,000 to 40,000:* Dell'Amore, C. 2014. "Beloved African Elephant Killed for Ivory." *National Geographic News,* June 16.

Part Two: Killer Whales

Chapter 13: Sea Rex

82 *intelligent, maternal, long-lived, cooperative:* Pitman, R. 2011. "An Introduction to the World's Premier Predator." *Whalewatcher* 40(1): 2–5.

Chapter 15: Super Social

93 *"no parallel outside humans":* Rendell, L., and H. Whitehead. 2001. "Culture in Whales and Dolphins." *Journal of Behavioral and Brain Science* 24(2): 309–82.

94 *"acceptance, approval, and peace":* Morton, *Listening to Whales,* p. 105.

94 *Dolphins who hear their own signature whistled:* King, S. L., and V. M. Janik. 2013. "Bottlenose Dolphins Can Use Learned Vocal Labels to Address Each Other." *PNAS* 110(32): 13216–21. See also Tyack, P. L., "Communication and Cognition," in *Biology of Marine Mammals,* p. 304, and Janik, V. M. 2013. "Cognitive Skills in Bottlenose Dolphin Communication." *Trends in Cognitive Sciences* 17(4): 157–59.

95 *Dolphins more than ten miles:* Janik, V. 2000. "Source Levels and the Estimated Active Space of Bottlenose Dolphin (*Tursiops truncatus*) Whistles in the Moray Firth, Scotland." *Journal of Comparative Physiology A* 186(7–8): 673–80.

95 *Atlantic spotted dolphins seemingly use:* Herzing, *Dolphin Diaries,* p. 103.

95 *When groups meet at sea:* Quick, N. J., and V. M. Janik. 2012. "Bottlenose Dolphins Exchange Signature Whistles When Meeting at Sea." *Proceedings of the Royal Society B* 279(1738): 2539–45.

95 *"an intriguing parallel":* Berg, K. S., et al. 2011. "Vertical Transmission of Learned Signatures in a Wild Parrot." *Proceedings of the Royal Society B* 279: 585–91.

95 *fairy wrens:* Morell, V. 2014. "A Rare Observation of Teaching in the Wild." *Science,* June 11.

Chapter 16: Singing and Sonar

98 Pituuu *and* Wee-oo-uuo*:* Morton, *Listening to Whales,* p. 117.

98 *ping-pong ball:* Tyack in *Biology of Marine Mammals,* pp. 291–92.

98 *four hundred clicks per* second: Ford and Ellis, *Transients,* p. 78.

Chapter 17: Diverse Minds

104 *balancing a newborn:* Morton, *Listening to Whales,* p. 139.

104 *"There is someone in there":* Vance, E. 2011. "It's Complicated: The Lives of Dolphins and Scientists." *Discover Magazine,* September 7.

Chapter 18: Brain Power

105 *nearly 20 percent:* Tyack in *Biology of Marine Mammals,* pp. 316–17.

106 the social brain: Ibid., pp. 316–17.

106 *Crozet Islands:* Guinet, C., and J. Bouvier. 1995. "Development of Intentional Stranding Hunting Techniques in Killer Whale (*Orcinus orca*) Calves at Crozet Archipelago." *Canadian Journal of Zoology* 73(1): 27–33.

107 *two killer whales teaching:* Matkin, C., and J. Durban. 2011. "Killer Whales in Alaskan Waters." *Whalewatcher* 40(1): 24–29.

107 *Atlantic spotted dolphin mothers:* Bender, C., D. Herzing, and D. Bjorklund. 2009. "Evidence of Teaching in Atlantic Spotted Dolphins (*Stenella frontalis*) by Mother Dolphins Foraging in the Presence of Their Calves." *Animal Cognition* 12(1): 43–53.

108 *bottlenose named Dolly:* Reiss, *Dolphin in the Mirror,* p. 169.

108 *Dolly* came up with the idea: Tyack in *Biology of Marine Mammals,* p. 315.

Chapter 19: Defying Explanation

110 *enveloped by fog:* Morton, *Listening to Whales,* pp. 113–15, 210.

112 *"Those whales saved my dog":* Ibid., pp. 93, 121.

113 *"They can read your mind":* Ibid., pp. 237–39, 97–98.

115 *"look through your otherness":* Parfit and Chisholm, *Lost Whale,* pp. 170–71.

115 *if a person remained aboard sleeping:* Ibid., p. 300.

115 *Luna was playing:* Ibid., pp. 99, 141, 143, 301.

116 *Karen Pryor* and *"Do something new":* Samuels, A., and P. L. Tyack, "Flukeprints: A History of Studying Cetacean Societies," in Mann et al., *Cetacean Societies,* p. 26. See also Reiss, *Dolphin in the Mirror,* p. 199.

117 *Akeakamai:* Reiss, *Dolphin in the Mirror,* p. 196.

118 *Photographer Bryant Austin:* Austin, B. 2013. *Beautiful Whales.* New York: Abrams. See also "Photographer Gets Up Close with Whales." 2013. *Here & Now,* June 3. http://hereandnow.wbur.org/2013/06/03/photographer-beautiful -whale.

Chapter 20: Helping in Mind

119 *"Just as the seal":* Pitman, R. L., and J. W. Durban. 2009. "Save the Seal!" *Natural History,* November.

121 *Don Pachico:* Don Pachico's interview can be viewed online in the "Destination Baja" episode of the PBS series *Saving the Ocean with Carl Safina,* available at PBS.org.

122 *On a sailboat off Venezuela:* Reiss, *Dolphin in the Mirror,* p. 207.

122 *"We were at least three miles":* Bearzi and Stanford, *Beautiful Minds,* pp. 25–26.

Chapter 21: The Cost of Captivity

Quotes for Garrett, Crowe, Ray, and Hargrove and some of the information on SeaWorld are from: Cowperthwaite, G., director and producer. 2013. *Blackfish.* DVD. Manny O Productions.

134 *"If she wasn't 'crying'":* Morton, *Listening to Whales,* p. 97.

Chapter 22: The Big Picture

136 *residents' diet is 65 percent:* Ford and Ellis, *Transients,* p. 26.

Epilogue

143 *"Anyone who studies a wild animal":* Morton, *Listening to Whales,* p. 5.

SELECTED BIBLIOGRAPHY

Bearzi, M., and C. B. Stanford. 2008. *Beautiful Minds: The Parallel Lives of Great Apes and Dolphins.* Cambridge, MA: Harvard University Press.

de Waal, F. 2013. *The Bonobo and the Atheist: In Search of Humanism Among the Primates.* New York: Norton.

Douglas-Hamilton, I., and O. Douglas-Hamilton. 1975. *Among the Elephants.* New York: Viking Books.

Ford, J.K.B., and G. M. Ellis. 1999. *Transients: Mammal-Hunting Killer Whales of British Columbia, Washington, and Southeastern Alaska.* Seattle: University of Washington Press.

Herzing, D. L. 2011. *Dolphin Diaries: My Twenty-Five Years with Spotted Dolphins in the Bahamas.* New York: St. Martin's Press.

Koch, C. 2012. *Consciousness: Confessions of a Romantic Reductionist.* Cambridge, MA: MIT Press.

Mann, J., R. C. Connor, P. L. Tyack, and H. Whitehead, eds. 2000. *Cetacean Societies: Field Studies of Dolphins and Whales.* Chicago: University of Chicago Press.

Morton, A. 2004. *Listening to Whales.* New York: Ballantine Books.

Moss, C., and M. Colbeck. 1993. *Echo of the Elephants: The Story of an Elephant Family.* New York: William Morrow.

Moss, C. J. 2000. *Elephant Memories: Thirteen Years in the Life of an Elephant Family.* Chicago: University of Chicago Press.

Moss, C. J., H. Croze, and P. Lee, eds. 2011. *The Amboseli Elephants: A Long-Term Perspective on a Long-Lived Mammal.* Chicago: University of Chicago Press.

Parfit, M., and S. Chisholm. 2013. *The Lost Whale: The True Story of an Orca Named Luna.* New York: St. Martin's Press.

Poole, J. 1997. *Coming of Age with Elephants: A Memoir.* New York: Voyageur Press.

Reiss, D. 2011. *The Dolphin in the Mirror: Exploring Dolphin Minds and Saving Dolphin Lives.* Boston: Houghton Mifflin Harcourt.

Tyack, P. L. 1999. "Communication and Cognition." In *Biology of Marine Mammals,* edited by J. E. Reynolds III and S. A. Rommel. Washington, DC: Smithsonian. pp. 287–323.

ACKNOWLEDGMENTS

Any recounting of kindnesses that went into helping me create this book will be inadequate and incomplete. But let me try: This book would not exist without the faith and diligence of Emily Feinberg and Roaring Brook Press. Reading about traumatized elephants while I was surrounded by dolphins in the Gulf of California made me ask myself a penetrating question whose answer formed the central concept for this book. For that fertile combination I thank author Gay Bradshaw and Brett Jenks of RARE Conservation. For exceptional help in understanding elephants, I owe Cynthia Moss, Iain Douglas-Hamilton, and Vicki Fishlock especially, along with Katito Sayialel, David Daballen, Daphne Sheldrick, Edwin Lusichi, Julius Shivegha, Gilbert Sabinga, Frank Pope, Shifra Goldenberg, George Wittemyer, Lucy King, Ike Leonard, Soila Sayialel, and Joseph Soltis. For crucial logistics that made my trip to Kenya click, Jean Hartley. For my killer whale immersion, I am deeply grateful to Ken Balcomb, Dave Ellifrit, Kathy Babiak, Bob Pitman, John Durban, Nancy Black, and Alexandra Morton.

Please consider contributing to Save the Elephants, the Amboseli Trust for Elephants, Big Life Foundation, the David Sheldrick Wildlife Trust, the Yellowstone Park Foundation, or the Center for Whale Research, each of which works on the front lines to keep these creatures with us.

On the editorial side, I thank the incomparable Jack Macrae, Jean Naggar, Jennifer Weltz, and Bonnie Thompson, skilled and faithful partners all. I'd like to humbly acknowledge the inspiration and encouragement I received for many years from Peter Matthiessen.

For material support, I thank especially Julie Packard, the Gilchrist Family, Andrew Sabin, Ann Hunter-Welborn and family, Susan O'Connor, Roy O'Connor, Robert Campbell, Beto Bedolfe, Glenda Menges, Sylvie Chantecaille, and others who prefer anonymity. For keeping us in business, Mayra Mariño.

For sharing life, spotting falcons, saving horseshoe crabs, closing in the chickens at night, and feeding everybody, I thank my wife, Patricia Paladines, in whom I've long recognized a deep reflection. What she sees in me, well—as you know, I'm not a mind reader.

Not least, of course, I thank Chula, Jude, Rosebud, Kane, Velcro, Emi, Maddox, Kenzie, and so many others, great and little, free-living, domesticated, and in between—who have opened my eyes. From doggies and furry orphans of our living room and yard to the great seabird colonies of remotest shores; the great fishes, turtles, and whales of deep, wide oceans; the hawks of autumn skies and the warblers of the springtime woods—to those in these pages and all the rest, I offer my delighted gratitude for bringing so much beauty, grace, love, joy, richness, heartache, dirt, mess, and mud into my life. In other words, for making it real.

Thanks, everybody.

Time to go. Bye.

INDEX

Leonard, Ike, 69

Luna (killer whale), 113–16

M

Maasai, 6–7, 13, 58

Macrae, Jack, 122

Madagascar, 48

Marineland of the Pacific, 112

Matthiessen, Peter, 1

Mayoral, Don Pachico, 121

Melville, Herman, 79

Mitani, John, 48

mongooses, 48–49

Morton, Alexandra, 93–94, 110–13, 133–34, 143

Moskito, James, 121

Moss, Cynthia, 3–9, 13–14, 39, 41–42, 46, 68, 72

N

names, animals' use of, 94–96

Namu (killer whale), 127

Natural Resources Defense Council, 137

Niimura, Yoshihito, 9

Nootka Sound, 113

O

octopus, 81

offshore killer whales, 87–88

orca, origin of term, 85

orcas, *see* killer whales

OrcaSound.net, 82

Orky (killer whale), 112, 133

P

Panksepp, Jaak, 19

Parfit, Michael, 115–16

parrots, 16, 95

Pitman, Bob, 119

poaching and ivory, 27–28, 57, 63–70

pods, *84*, 86, 91–93

Poole, Joyce, 43, 45

primates

chimpanzees, 48

gorillas, 14

lemurs, 48–49

vervet monkeys, 55

Pryor, Karen, 116

Puget Sound, 136